The Grace Race

Mo Mydlo

DEDICATION

I would like to dedicate this book to some of my amazing teachers of The Word of God; Creflo Dollar, Joyce Meyer, Beth Moore, Kenneth Copeland, Jodi Vermaas, and Justin Miller. The daily study that I have received under your teaching has brought peace, joy, and strength into my life in a way that I could never explain in words. I love The Word of God because of all of you. I thank you.

Stay in The Race, Relying
Heavily on Grace!

ACKNOWLEDGMENTS

I want to thank my sweet husband Tommy for always encouraging my writing and my teaching. You are a shining example to men of how a husband should treat his bride. Your humility is enchanting.

I want to thank my kids for loving me the way that you do. You are all becoming such amazing witnesses for Jesus and there is no greater joy for a mother than to see her children abiding in the light.

I want to thank my Mom for always being there to edit my books and encourage my writing. I want to thank my Dad for showing me how to accept The Father's love correctly. You have always been my hero. I want to thank my Mother- in- law and Father- in -law for raising such a wonderful son. He is my prince and my partner for life.

1.
Your God Shaped Hole

For many years, I was lost in a world of chronic anxiety and perfectionism and it has only been my walk with Jesus that has granted me peace. This kind of peace is mentioned in the scriptures as "the peace that passes understanding". That means, you don't even know why you feel peace, you just do. That is Jesus! He is The Prince of Peace!

From everything that I have learned about "real life" and not just the superficial life that people will allow others to see; I know there are so many hurts going on, just in the few eyes that will read this book. There are so many of you struggling with doubts, fears, depression, anxiety, shame and guilt. There is no doubt that many of you that are studying this book are on your last leg. I am here to tell you, there is no pit too deep that our God cannot reach in and pull you out of.

Each one of us was born imperfect. We were born with what I like to call our "God shaped hole". We yearn for something all of the time. For some of us, this yearning is a habit, a drug, maybe an addiction. For some of us, it is a guilt from the past that we cannot seem to let go of. For some it is an insecurity that the world will eventually figure out how broken we are. For some of us, it is the fear of the unknown, an attempt to control everything around us including our loved ones to hide this hole from the world. We don't want to be exposed, right?

God knows. He sees your mess. He made you. He knows what you struggle with. He knows what sin you succumb to. He knows you may marry the wrong person, pick up that drug that you shouldn't, spend that money in the checkbook when you know there is none to spend. .He knows everything my friend, and He loves us anyways.

The bible says: "While we were still sinners Christ died for us." When we think about the President and who he puts around him, he has to hire people that would stand in the way of a bullet for him. That makes sense because he is the president right? He is an important person in the world's eyes. He couldn't be replaced easily. But why in the world would anyone die for us? We are flawed, imperfect, and sinful. That's what we think; but the truth is, we have just believed lies for too long.

We believe lies, we trust our feelings; we know what we have done and where we have fallen short; and we don't believe there is anyone that could forgive us. Therefore we hide in our sin. However God sees us and he sees our sins and He loves us anyways. God is crazy about you.-yes, you! He desires a personal and intimate relationship with each one of us so intensely that He sent his Son to earth, knowing that His flesh and blood would have to go to the cross to give His life for us because of our sins.

Here is the truth. We all are going to die one day. We all know that, but do you know that this life isn't everything? We will spend eternity somewhere. It is one of two places-Heaven or Hell. Take one bit of advice from me my friend, choose Heaven.

Our good works can't get us into Heaven. There is no deed good enough. There is no: "I'm a good person." Because the truth is, we sin every day and we need forgiveness every day. If there was any other way to get to Heaven than for Jesus to pay that penalty on the cross for us, God would never have sacrificed His Son.

Jesus is the way, the truth and the life. No one comes to the Father, without Jesus. He is the gift... He is supposed to be the one to fill that God shaped hole. There is no man, no habit, no amount of money, no amount of shopping, no amount of laughing, no amount of wine, no amount of financial stability, no perfect vacations, and no perfect children. NOTHING will fill that void in your life like Jesus can. These other options will only keep you wanting more.

I love what Beth Moore says about sin. "There is nothing that sin can add to your life, that can replace what it takes from you." Did you hear that? Nothing that sin gives us can replace what it takes away. The devil has lied to us long enough, and it is time to hear the truth. The truth is, we need Jesus! He's the answer to all of our prayers. He's that one thing that we don't even know that we are craving, we just are. He's the one thing. He's the everything. He's the beginning and the end. He formed us in our mother's womb, and He will be there when we take our last breath. Do not let that last breath be the first time that you recognize Him as Savior. At that point, it will be too late. The Word says; "Every knee will bow, and every tongue will confess that Jesus is Lord." I pray that you confess it today.

Jeremiah 29:11 says; "For I know that plans that I have for you says the Lord, plans to prosper you and not to harm you, plans to give you hope, and a future." My friend, God's plan for our lives is nothing short of amazing. When we finally submit to His plans, and not ours, we become truly free. His love is for us.

If you have been abused: His love is for you.

If you have been abusive: His love is for you.

If you have been addicted: His love is for you.

If you are addicted right now: His love is for you.

If you are married: His love is for you.

If you have been abandoned: His love is for you.

If you are living with someone outside of marriage: His love is for you.

If you have been in prison: His love is for you.

If you are imprisoned with fear and doubt and shame: His love is for you.

If you are in abundance: His love is for you.

If you are in lack: His love is for you.

I you are healthy or sick: His love is for you.

If you still have breath: His love is for you.

My friend, Jesus came to bind up the broken hearted and to set the captives free.

I know I am going to Heaven someday, not because of anything I have done, because my best works here on earth are like filthy rags in God's eyes. But, I am secure in my eternal destination because Jesus is my everything. He paid the price for me, and I will someday live with Him in Glory! And this promise is available to you as well and anyone who chooses to make Him Lord of their life.

Today, will you open that gift, that perfect gift of forgiveness and peace that Jesus has for you? That gift has been sitting there for years just waiting to be opened. He gave His life so that we can approach the throne of our God, clean and new.

Isaiah 61: 1-3 reads; "The Spirit of the Sovereign Lord is on me, because The Lord has anointed me to preach good news to the poor. He has sent me to bind up the broken hearted, to proclaim freedom for the captives, and release from darkness for the prisoners, to proclaim the year of the Lord's favor, and the day of vengeance of our God. To comfort all who mourn, and provide for those who grieve in Zion-To bestow on them a crown of beauty instead of ashes, the oil of gladness instead of mourning, and a garment of praise instead of a spirit of despair. They will be called Oaks of Righteousness, a planting of the Lord for the display of His splendor."

This message is for us my friend, all of us. Won't you allow Him to be your comforter, your provider, your deliverer from your darkness? I opened up that gift 15 years ago, and I have never looked back. I know now, that there is no condemnation for those that are in Christ Jesus

The first step in your healing of any kind is a personal relationship with Jesus. If you feel in your heart that now is the time to get right with Him, then do it now! Now is the time to break free from these chains that have held you for so long. Don't wait. Do it today. You'll never be the same.

Let's Study A Little About Salvation:

Read the following scriptures:

- Romans 10:9-10
  - John 3:16
  - John 5:24
  - John 14:6
- Ephesians 2:8-9
  - Acts 2:21
  - Acts 2:38-39

Journal a Prayer to God thanking Him for saving you, or asking Him to save you; Today is the day!

What If?

Posted on September 9, 2013 by momydlo@wordpress.com

After 40 years of living in a mind that naturally goes to the "What ifs" I think today God took me through the same questioning Spirit, but not in a tormenting, worrisome way, as I am used to fighting with Spiritual warfare and The Word of God. Now I proceed in a way that may lead someone who needs to hear the truth, to finally start seeking that truth.

What if? What if you have spent your entire life here on earth accumulating wealth, or prestige, or a stature that men deem as having arrived? And, then….you still feel empty. What then?

What if? What if you have worked your body like a machine, eating healthy, exercising, training and disciplining yourself to the point of "perfection" or what the world calls "perfection"? And, then…you still feel like something is missing. What then?

What if? What if you have been a diligent saver, money manager and investor and you have all of your children's college paid for, inheritance accounted for, and weddings paid in advance? But…you realize you still don't feel secure.

What if? What if you have pursued your "bucket list" (your list of things that you want to do before you die)? You have travelled and seen the wonders of the world, the majesty of mountains, oceans, valleys, deserts, and every other sight that you just "Must see" and you have tried all of the dangerous, risky death defying things that you can think of. But, you still feel like there is something that you haven't done.

What if? What if you have provided for the poor, given to charities, attended benefits and really expensive dinners that are designed for causes that are amazing? But, you still feel like the guilt for your bad mistakes just won't go away, no matter how much good you try to do. What if? What if you think to yourself if I just stay busy enough, working, playing, planning, checking off lists and planning for the future I will be able to quiet these nagging anxious thoughts that I deal with every day; like "what if this happens" or "if only that hadn't happened"? However it seems like these thoughts just will never go away? What if?

I bet you can relate to one or many of the above if you live in this world, and you obviously live in this world or you wouldn't be reading this blog. Do you know how I know? Because it is the gospel truth. You see- if you keep searching and striving and stretching and reaching for the one thing that you think will fill that emptiness inside you that you just can't explain; you will never truly feel full. Why? Because that hole that you have in your heart, is designed to allow only one thing to fill it... God! It's your God shaped hole that we are all created with. You see, God made us to need Him. He made us to be desperate for Him. Why? Because He loves us so much that He couldn't help Himself. He has always desired a love relationship with us, and when we deny Him that, and we settle for cheap substitutes, we always feel empty.

Let's just go a little bit further with our "What ifs", just because Hey, maybe I may never get you this far in a blog about salvation so I better push it when I get you. What if? What if you say it's all a farce? You decide that these Jesus freaks are all a bunch of wimpy, complaining, can't -do -anything on- their -own, so they need a Savior to cast all of their anxiety upon because they just need to wake up and smell reality? What if you have said; "No thanks I am going my own way. I don't need a God to call on. I make my own destiny?" And, let's go one more step; what if you teach your way to your children, because you don't want them mislead, and believing myths and fantasies. You have taught your children to be hard working, "good people" believing in only this maybe 70-100 years of life that they are given until they die forever. And, What if you are wrong?

What if you have decided to go the atheistic way, deciding to just live and try to make the best of this life, teaching this kind of belief to your children; and you end up wrong? What if, these Jesus freaks who say that if you make Jesus Lord of your life and follow Him you will go to Heaven and live a life of pure joy in The Presence of The Lord and loved ones that have gone before you who believed? And they say that you will never experience tears or sadness or sorrow ever again, only supernatural health, happiness and complete restoration; What if they turn out to be right?

But more than this; what if these crazy Christians are right and you never figure this out while on this side of death, and you do actually go to Hell? There you might experience eternal separation from other people, from any light, in total darkness, constant pain, suffering, agony that NEVER ENDS! But more importantly, what if you led your family that way? I don't know if we could even fathom that "what if" as parents? Can we?

I guess I felt led to say this today for no other reason than... I care. I care about you. I care about your kids. I care about your eternity. And, guess what? If we Christians are wrong....we have nothing to lose, we lived a life of hope, peace, joy, knowing that we were going to a better place than here. But, I am sad to say that if you are not choosing to believe, you have everything to lose.

Today, if you have even the slightest twinge in your gut that something that I have written is truth: may I please offer for you prayer? I pray that you decide right now to bend a knee to the only way to Heaven... Jesus Christ. Because here's a fact: The Word says, "One day, every knee will bow and every tongue will confess that Jesus is Lord." Choose to make Him Lord on this side of death. He truly is the only cure for what ails you. I love you too much not to say it, my friend, JESUS IS LORD!
What if?

Let's Study A Little About Hell:

Read the following scriptures:

- Matthew 25:31-46

- 2 Thessalonians 1:1-12

- Jude 5-7

- Journal a Prayer to God thanking Him that because of a personal relationship with Jesus Christ; and because you have made Jesus Lord of your life, you have escaped the torment of an eternity in a very real Hell.

God's Diverse Family

Posted on December 30, 2012 by momydlo@wordpress.com

Yesterday my husband and I hosted a post-funeral reception at our home for a dear friend of ours whose husband passed right before Christmas. We were blessed to welcome over 60 people for lunch and fellowship in The Lord. God is so good. It had been raining all night long, and while I was in the shower I prayed that God would stop the rain so we could utilize the outside of our home for some of the hosting. God answered my prayer. The sun came out just before the guests arrived.

Towards the end of the reception I found myself on my back porch visiting with three people who conversing there. We began speaking of where we were when God called us, how His love changed us, and what kind of passion we have to share that love and grace with others. We spoke of miracles we have witnessed, changed lives we have been able to encounter, and the expectation of our home in Heaven.

I didn't want the moment to end. I felt God all over this moment as I looked around at each member there. I realized that we were confessing fears to each other; encouraging each other in the difficult walk that we must walk sometimes as Christ followers; and truly loving each other as brothers and sisters in Christ.

Then God really showed me something. He said; "Mo, look at each other. Look who I love". I realized that the four of us sitting there consisted of me (a once mean girl in high school who cared about myself more than anyone else, and didn't treat others as kind as I should); a US Marshall who confessed to being a once very angry man, until God softened his heart; a tattoo artist who couldn't stop smiling because of his love towards God; and an author who had died and gone to Hell twice and begged to come back to earth to share about Jesus' grace with everyone. Yes, the four of us were the oddest small group I had ever witnessed. And, yet, I felt like we were family.

Hurrah for the love of a Father who sees nothing but the hearts of His children. He sees lives that He can be glorified in. He sees past what the world sees. I am eternally grateful and honored to be part of such a diverse family. Yes, God is the redeemer of earthly vessels that would have been destined to an eternal life absent of His glory. He is our Redeemer! Thank you Daddy for my awesome family.

Let's Study A Little About Heaven:

Read the following scriptures:

- John 14:2

- Revelation 22:1-5

- Revelation 21:4

- Revelation 21:22-27

- Luke 23:43

- Journal a prayer to God thanking Him for the eternal home that He has prepared for you in Heaven, and the beautiful diverse family that will be with you. Thank you Jesus!

You Are Clean!

Posted on November 21, 2012 by momydlo@wordpress.com

I am loving reading the book of Acts in my quiet time with The Lord. It is such an awesome history book of the early church. Each day I am introduced to a new character that God decided would help start his church. Today I was amazed (as usual) at what God showed Peter and how relevant it is to us today.

While praying one night on the roof, Peter (who was hungry) saw a vision. It was of something like a large sheet coming down from Heaven covering four-footed animals, beasts, reptiles, fish, and birds, and God told him; "Get up Peter. Kill and eat."

Peter (who was raised according to the old Hebraic law) replied; "surely not, Lord! Nothing impure or unclean has ever entered my mouth". Well, then comes the second voice from Heaven......And, here is what I believe was God's main command to him; "Do not call anything impure that God has made clean."

My friends, it was time for God to show His glory, His forgiveness and His mercy to the Gentile nation as well as the Jewish nation. The Gentile nation was everyone who wasn't a Jew. We see Peter, an integral part of a Divine visit in which the Holy Spirit is poured out on a Roman Centurion named Cornelius and a room full of uncircumcised believers. Peter baptized them, shared this experience with the other disciples and they realized that "God has granted even the Gentiles repentance into life".

The Grace Race

Amen and Amen, thank you Jesus that you came for the Jews and for the Gentiles. You loved all of us enough that you wouldn't allow us to die in our sin. We are the Gentiles my friends. We are also Unforsaken!

But, why do we forget so quickly that we are clean! Why do we forget so quickly what God told Peter; "Do not call anything unclean that God has made clean." Why do we still feel so guilty over sins of our past, that we have confessed and repented for, and maybe even over and over and over? How dare we be like Peter and say; "Surely not Lord!"

I felt God say that to me this morning; "Mo, Do not call yourself impure. I have made you clean". Sometimes I allow the Devil to have just an extra second too long in my thinking, and he tries to dirty up the clean chalk board that God has already erased. He tries to put those ugly old grave clothes back on my new fresh body. Until I confess out loud to him and to myself; "No, I am clean!"

This is why we must renew our minds daily in the truths that God has written and saved for us on the pages of His Word. Because we will automatically start listening to the old ugly nature again if we don't allow our new man to reign. We have to give our new nature the honor and the glory and the authority that He deserves. After all; "He is greater in me, than that which is in the world".

You are clean my friend! Stop letting the devil tell you otherwise!

Let's Study A Little About Being Washed Clean By The Blood of Christ:

- Read the following scriptures:

- Ephesians 5:26-27

- Hebrews 9:11-15

- Hebrews 10:19-23

- 2 Peter 1:5-9

- Journal a prayer to God thanking Him that the blood of Jesus cleansed you of your sins once and for all at the time of your conversion:

2.

LIVING AND LOVING ON PURPOSE

Are You Committed?

I love The Book of Ruth because I believe we all have so many lessons that we can learn from our sister Ruth. Ruth had a truly divine gift of living purposely. She took every decision seriously and she made such a huge impact while she was here. I believe we need to glean some knowledge from her as we walk out our days here on earth.

My hope for you is that you develop such an insatiable thirst for more and more of the Word of God that it becomes the great obsession in your life. I know that it has for me. I am especially excited to study an Old Testament lesson together because we sometimes think as modern day new covenant believers that the New Testament is all that we need to apply to our lives. But, the truth is; Jesus is all over the Old Testament. And, these Old Testament Heroes did such amazing things without the forgiveness and grace of the cross that we experience now. We should have no problem living out the same sort of pursuit of holiness and excellence that they do. After all, we have The Holy Spirit now. Jesus himself was raised under the Hebrew law and He made sure that we all know that He didn't come to abolish the law but to fulfill it.

Ruth Chapter 1
"In the days when the judges ruled, there was a famine in the land, and a man from Bethlehem in Judah, together with his wife and two sons, went to live for a while in the country of Moab. The man's name was Elimelech, his wife's name was Naomi, and the names of his two sons were Mahlon and Kilion. They were Ephrathites from Bethlehem, Judah. And they went to Moab and lived there.
Now Elimelech, Naomi's husband, died, and she was left with her two sons. They married Moabite women, one named Orpah and the other Ruth. After they had lived there about ten years, both Mahlon and Kilion also died, and Naomi was left without her two sons and her husband.
When she heard in Moab that the Lord had come to the aid of his people by providing food for them, Naomi and her daughters-in-law prepared to return home from there. With her two daughters-in-law she left the place where she had been living and set out on the road that would take them back to the land of Judah.
Then Naomi said to her daughters-in-law, "Go back, each of you to your mother's home. May the Lord show kindness to you, as you have shown to your dead and me. May the

Lord grant that each of you will find rest in the home of another husband." Then she kissed them and they wept aloud and said to her, "We will go back with you to your people." But Naomi said; "Return home my daughters. Why would you come with me? Am I going to have any more sons, who could become your husbands? Return home my daughters; I am too old to have another husband. Even if I thought there was still hope for me-even if I had a husband tonight and gave birth to sons- would you wait until they grow up? Would you remain unmarried for them? No, my daughters. It is more bitter for me than for you, because The Lord's hand has gone out against me!"

At this they wept again. Then Orpah kissed her mother-in-law good-by, but Ruth clung to her.

"Look", said Naomi, "your sister-in-law is going back to her people and her gods. Go back with her."

But Ruth replied, "Don't urge me to leave you or to turn back from you. Where you go I will go, and where you stay I will stay. Your people will be my people and your God my God. Where you die I will die, and there I will be buried. May the Lord deal with me, be it ever so severely, if anything but death separates you and me." When Naomi realized that Ruth was determined to go with her, she stopped urging her.

So the two women went on until they came to Bethlehem. When they arrived in Bethlehem, the whole town was stirred because of them, and the women exclaimed, "Can this be Naomi?"

"Don't call me Naomi," she told them. "Call me Mara, because The Almighty has made my life very bitter. I went away full, but the Lord has brought me back empty. Why call me Naomi? The Lord has afflicted me; The Almighty has brought misfortune upon me."

So Naomi returned from Moab accompanied by Ruth the Moabites, her daughter-in-law, arriving in Bethlehem as the barley harvest was beginning.

Here we find three women-now widows, and at a crossroads in life. Naomi had given her two daughter-in-laws her blessing for them to return to their hometowns, and families. They were not bound to each other by marriage vows or contracts anymore. Death ended that. But we see that the two ladies made two very different choices.

Let's talk about Orpah first. Orpha did what most women, if we are being honest, would do. She decided to return home. I'm sure she loved her mother-in-law. It says they wept when they left each other, however she decided to go home to her family. We usually go home to Mom and Dad right?

I know when my husband and I were newlyweds and we would have an argument; I was drawn to my mom's house. I needed that cup of coffee at her kitchen table, and needed to vent about how Tommy was driving me crazy, and that this marriage thing was hard. Because as much as my mother-in-law loves me, it really doesn't matter how wrong Tommy is in the situation, she will defend him-because he still is her baby boy. I understand that now. I have teenage boys. So, if I wanted the support that I desired, I would go and visit Mom.

Orpah went home, but Ruth decided to stay. She not only decided to stay; she made a covenant with God that if she walks away from Naomi, God can deal with her however He sees fit. In verse 17 she says; *"May The Lord deal with me, be it ever so severely, if anything but death separates you and me."* That is bold! That is brave! That is Commitment!

The first requirement for living and loving on purpose is commitment. Commitment says; "No matter the cost-no matter the circumstances-no matter the outcome, I'm in this."

This world that we live in is so void of commitment. We stay married until we just don't feel it anymore. We buy cars and treat them with such care and concern for a couple weeks. Then when they aren't new anymore, we throw fast food wrappers and receipts all over and rarely run it through the carwash. We ground our kids for misbehavior, and then when we are sick of hearing them complain about their consequences, we lift the grounding and let them do what they want.

Where is the kind of commitment that says; *"Your people will be my people, your God my God, where you die, I will die?"*

Our commitment as modern day believers must be rooted and grounded in trust. We must trust that God will be very near to us when we choose to do the hard things. We have to trust that if we choose to follow through on promises and covenants that we have the strength in our relationship with Jesus Christ to help see us through. Commitment is doing the hard things. But, praise God that we know God lives among the hard things and not the easy ones.

Our God is a God that stays very close to the broken hearted. Our God is a God who bears the burdens of His children. Our God is a God who allows us to cast our cares and concerns on Him. Our God can be trusted

For several years I led a repair and renovation ministry for people in need in the community. We would do three day makeovers for individuals who couldn't afford to pay for the repairs that they needed done on their homes. It was a joy. I was blessed to lead over 100 projects, almost 1000 volunteers and a team of leaders who are still some of my closest friends today.

But, nothing taught me true commitment like promising the recipient that when they returned to their home on Sunday afternoon; that the two hundred or so volunteers that trampled through their home all weekend fixing, repairing, cleaning, decorating, you name it; will be outside waiting for them to drive in and enjoy their perfect home that we created for them.

Believe me; accidents happened. Black paint was spilled on white carpet, homeowner's belongings that we tried to keep safe somehow disappeared in the chaos, septic tanks backed up, main breakers were tripped for the electrical, and water pipes burst. But, none of this mattered where our reveal was concerned. All of the volunteers, the neighbors, the church members and most importantly the homeowner expected the reveal to go off without a hitch. And, guess what? It always did. Well, almost always. Out of the over 100 projects that I led, we had three late reveals. Not bad right?

I can only attribute this record to my never-ending commitment to the task at hand, to the schedule we set, but especially to God. People would look at me and say; "Mo, why don't we just come back in a few days and…." Or, "Mo, maybe we should just call the homeowner and say that we couldn't do this" Or, "Mo, it's ok if we postpone it a little." But, I never would. I truly just kept pushing and praying and loving on workers until the job would finish. I think it was kind of an unspoken little promise between God and me that if I would keep focused and committed, He would show up with the supernatural power to pull off what only He can do. And, He always did! It was a really fun job! But, I have to admit writing books and messages in the air conditioning at the computer sure beats sewage back-ups.

Are you committed? Are you like Ruth or Orpah? Will you stand in the gap for those you love, even if it means sacrificing to do so? I want to encourage you to never give up on your commitment to Christ.

Let's study a little about commitment.

Read the following passages:

- Psalm 37:1-6

- Matthew 10: 17-42

- Matthew 16:21-28

- Journal a prayer to God asking Him to give you a fresh desire to grow in your commitment to Him.

2.

Living And Loving On Purpose
Go The Extra Mile

Ruth Chapter 2

Now Naomi had a relative on her husband's side, from the clan of Elimelech. , a man of standing, who name was Boaz. And Ruth the Maoabitess said to Naomi, "Let me go to the fields and pick up the leftover grain behind anyone in whose eyes I may find favor." Naomi said to her, "Go ahead, my daughter." So she went out and began to glean in the fields behind the harvesters. As it turned out, she found herself working in a field belonging to Boaz, who was from the clan of ?Elimelech. Just then Boaz arrived from Bethlehem and greeted the harvesters, "The Lord be with you."

"The Lord bless you!:" they called back..Boaz asked the foreman of his harvesters, "Whose young woman is that?" The foreman replied, "She is the Moabitess who came back from Moab with Naomi. She said, 'Please let me glean and gather among the sheaves behind the harvesters.' She went into the field and has worked steadily from morning until now, except a short rest in the shelter."

So Boaz said to Ruth,"My daughter, listen to me. Don't go and glean in another field where the men are harvesting, and follow along after the girls. I have told the men not to touch you. And whenever you are thirsty, go and get a drink from the water jars the men have filled. "

At this she bowed with her face to the ground. She exclaimed, "Why have I found such favor in your eyes that you notice me-a foreigner?" Boaz replied; "I've been told all about what you have done for your mother-in-laws since the death of your husband- how you left your father and mother and your homeland and came to live with a people you did not know before. May the Lord repay you for what you have done. May you be richly rewarded by The Lord, The God of Israel under whose wings, you have come to take refuge."

"May I continue to find favor in your eyes, my lord", she said. "You have given me comfort and have spoken kindly to your servant-though I do not have the standing of one of our servant girls."

At mealtime Boaz said to her; "Come over here. Have some bread and dip it in the wine vinegar." When she sat down with the harvesters, he offered her some roasted grain. She had all that she wanted and had some left over. AS she got up to glean, Boaz gave order to his men. "Even if she gathers among the sheaths don't embarrass her. Rather pull out some stalks for her from the bundles and leave them for her to pick up, and don't rebuke her."

So Ruth gleaned in the field until evening. Then she threshed the barley she had gathered and it amounted to about an ephah. She carried it back to town and her mother-in-law saw how much she had gathered. Ruth also brought out and gave her what she had left over after she had left over after she had eaten enough.

Her mother-in-law asked her, "Where did you glean today?" Where did you work? Blessed is the man who took notice of you. Then Ruth told her mother-in-law about the one at whose place she had been working. "The name of the man I worked with today is Boaz." she said. "The Lord bless him!" Naomi said to her daughter-in-law. "He has not stopped showing kindness to the living and the dead." She added; "That man is one of our relatives, he is one of our kinsman-redeemers." Then Ruth the Moabitess said; "He even said to me, 'stay with my workers until they finish harvesting all of my grain."

Naomi said to Ruth her daughter-in-law, "It will be good for you, my daughter, to go with his girls, because in someone else's field you might be harmed." So Ruth stayed close to the servant girls of Boaz to glean until the barley and wheat harvests were finished. And she lived with her mother-in-law.

Here we meet Boaz…Boaz entered the scene and we are quickly shown that He is a believer. We recognize that he is a believer by the way he greeted his servants; "The Lord be with you." But, we are assured that he is a believer by how he acts. We can tell the world all day long that we are Christians, but God wants us to act like Christians. Sometimes we can do more harm than good for The Kingdom, by wearing that Jesus shirt, then losing our patience or acting like a jerk.

Not Boaz!

Boaz spoke kindly to his servants, he welcomed Ruth, who was an outsider, and he strictly followed the laws that were put in place to provide for the poor; gleaning. Gleaning means; "Handfuls on purpose". The Israelite law that helped provide food for the poor was gleaning. The harvesters would purposely leave a portion of wheat behind for the poor to come and pick up so they could be provided for.

Boaz not only talked the talk, he walked the walk. Which brings me to my second point of living and loving on purpose.

Living and loving purposely requires that we go the extra mile.

Jesus is serious about us going the extra mile. In Matthew 5:40-41; He says: "If someone sues you and takes your tunic, give him your cloak as well. If someone forces you to go one mile, go with him two miles".

Boaz went the extra mile. He not only allowed Ruth to glean in his fields, he told the other men to stay away from her. He invited her and her mother- in-law to get drinks from their water jars whenever they needed them, and he invited her to dine with him at meal times.

But, my favorite thing that Boaz did; I believe showed his true soft heart. He told the men; "If she gleans incorrectly, don't embarrass her." My friend, he was already caring for her heart.

We are called as Christians to go the extra mile. If we could just get it the way Boaz got it, we could be so effective for the Kingdom. We are God's plan A, and there is no plan B. We are the ones that are called to carry the gospel of Jesus Christ to a hurting world. We have to take this call seriously, and we can't do it effectively if we aren't willing to go the extra mile. We have to be ok sometimes going places that aren't in our comfort zone, welcome people that might not look like you or me and lean in towards the people that God cares seriously about; the hurting and the lost.

My friend, if we don't go that extra mile with our neighbors, our work associates, our unsaved friends, they may never hear of the saving power of Jesus Christ.

I am not so far from my past life that did not include Jesus that I forget how unhappy I was, how selfish I was and how desperate I longed for some sort of purpose for my life. I don't want that for anyone. It is God's will that none shall perish, but **all** shall have eternal life.

It's our job as disciples of Jesus Christ to go above and beyond to hit the **ALL** that God is talking about.. Living and Loving on purpose requires us to go above and beyond!

Going above and beyond means; being the first to apologize and ask for forgiveness when you have had an argument with someone, especially your husband or kids. Going above and beyond means stopping whatever task you are in the middle of, when you see that it is obvious that someone you encounter needs a gentle or kind word from you, or maybe some love. Going above and beyond means putting others needs before yours; even when your flesh is screaming; *"What about me?" What about me? What about me?"* Going above and beyond is living and loving on purpose.

Are you willing to live like Boaz and go above and beyond to reach the lost world for Jesus?

Let's study a little about going the extra mile.

Read the following passages:

- Mark 16:15

- Matthew 5:38-42

- Matthew 28:16-20

- 1 Peter 1:15-16

- Journal a prayer to God asking Him to help you go the extra mile for Him.

2.

Living And Loving On Purpose
Obedience, No Matter What

Let's move into chapter three of Ruth. We find that Boaz is what the bible refers to as a Kinsman Redeemer to the women. A Kinsman Redeemer was a relative that volunteered to take responsibility for the extended family when a woman's husband died. Boaz had already taken some responsibility for these women by allowing them to glean in his fields; let's read on.

Ruth Chapter 3

One day Naomi her mother-in-law said to her; "My daughter, should I not try to find a home for you, where you will be well provided for? Is not Boaz, with whose servant girls you have been, a kinsman of ours? Tonight he will be winnowing barley on the threshing floor, Wash and perfume yourself, and put on your best clothes. Then go down to the threshing floor, but don't let him know you are there until after he has finished eating and drinking. When he lies down, note the place where he is lying. Then go and uncover his feet and lie down. He will tell you what to do."

"I will do whatever you say", Ruth answered. So she went down to the threshing floor and did everything her mother-in-law told her to do. When Boaz had finished eating and drinking and was in good spirits, he went over to lie down. In the middle of the night something startled the man, and he turned and discovered a woman lying at his feet. "Who are you?" he asked. I am your servant Ruth," she said. "Spread the corner of your garment over me since you are a kinsman-redeemer."

"The Lord bless you, my daughter," he replied. "This kindness is greater than that which you showed earlier; you have not run after the younger men, whether rich or poor. And now, my daughter, don't be afraid. I will do for you all that you ask. All my fellow townsmen know that you are a woman of noble character. Although it is true that I am near of kin, there is a kinsman-redeemer nearer than I. Stay here for the night, and in the morning if he wants to redeem, good; let him redeem. But if he is not willing, as surely as the Lord lives I will do it. Lie here until morning."

So she lay at his feet until morning, but got up before anyone could be recognized; and he said; "Don't let it be known that a woman came to the threshing floor."

He also said; "Bring me the shawl you are wearing and hold it out." When she did so, he poured into it six measures of barley and put it on her. Then he went back to town.

When Ruth came to her mother-in-law, Naomi asked, "How did it go my daughter?" Then she told her everything Boaz had done for her and added, "He gave me these six measures of barley, saying, 'Don't go back to your mother-in-law empty-handed." Then Naomi said, "Wait, my daughter, until you find out what happens. For the man will not rest until the matter is settled today."

I don't know about you, but the first time I read this I thought; *I know I'm a country girl*, but I couldn't help but hear Reba Macintyre singing: "Here's your one chance Fancy don't let me down." Side note; if you haven't heard this one, it's a classic!

Until I studied it more and realized that it was customary for a servant to lie at her master's feet and even share a part of his covering. By doing this, it was Ruth's way of letting Boaz know that he could become her kinsman redeemer; that he could find someone to marry her, or marry her himself.

I think the nice perfume and pretty clothes were just a little special touch. You know we know cute right friend? We don't wear our ugly sweat pants out on that first date!!!!

I think the biggest lesson we learn from this chapter is obedience. Ruth doesn't even question Naomi's suggestions, she just obeys. She doesn't say; "Well, I'd like to play the field a little, keep my options open, before I tie myself down to one guy." No, she simply obeys. She shows us the third aspect to living and loving on purpose. It is to be obedient, no matter the call.

God may be calling you to do something that seems so out of your character, your comfort zone, and it may not even make natural sense to you. But, I am going to tell you, God isn't involved in the natural. He is supernatural. His ways are not our ways.

I was walking with my husband one day, and I said to him. It is almost as if God said to me one day; "Can you just do what I call you to do? Don't ask questions, just do it". Ladies, God doesn't need us to understand what HE is doing, He just needs us to obey. It's like when our kids say; "Why?" And, what do we answer? "Because I said so, that's why."

He blesses us by allowing us to be part of His plan. He is God. He could stop this whole mess called life at any time; instead He equips us to lead others to HIM. God is constantly looking for hearts that will just do what He says.

We are still those sinners in the garden choosing to eat from the tree of good and evil, when He is just calling us to eat from the tree of life!

In 2Chronicles 16:9 it reads; "For the eyes of the Lord range throughout the earth to strengthen hearts that are fully committed to Him". He is looking my friend. He is searching the entire earth to find some willing servants, that HE can grow up and use.

Obedience at any cost is the only bumper sticker that every Christian should have on their car. God's word says; "If you love me, you will obey my commands". We love Him right? Then we need to take a lesson from Ruth and just do what God and our Spiritual authorities tell us to do.

God takes Spiritual authority very seriously. If He chooses to use you to shepherd others, like He did Naomi, be prepared, because He will keep you accountable too. I am sold out for Jesus, completely enamored with Him, hopelessly devoted to Him, and forever indebted to Him, and my call sign on my life is;

Isaiah 26:8:"Yes, LORD, walking in the way of your laws, we wait for you; your name and renown are the desire of our hearts".

It is the desire of my heart that Jesus is made famous because of my obedience. Living and loving on purpose requires obedience at any cost! Are you willing to obey God with whatever He calls you to do?

Let's study a little about obedience at any cost:

Read the following passages:

- Deuteronomy 28:1-2

- Joshua 24:24

- Luke 11:28

- Philippians 2:5-11

- Journal a prayer to God asking Him to help you to obey Him no matter what the call.

2.

Living and Loving on Purpose

Taking Godly Risks And Trusting God With The Outcome

Ruth Chapter 4

Meanwhile Boaz went up to the town gate and sat there. When the kinsman-redeemer he had mentioned came along, Boaz said, "Come over here, my friend, and sit down." So he went over and sat down. Boaz took ten of the elders of the town and said, "Sit here," and they did so.

Then he said to the kinsman-redeemer, "Naomi, who has come back from Moab, is selling the piece of land that belonged to our brother Elimelech. I thought I should bring the matter to your attention and suggest that you buy it in the presence of these seated here and in the presence of the elders of my people,. If you will redeem it, do so. But if you will not, tell me, so I will know. For no one has the right to do it except you, and I am next in line."

"I will redeem it," he said. Then Boaz said, "On the day you buy the land from Naomi and from Ruth the Moabitess, you acquire the dead man's widow, in order to maintain the name of the dead with his property."

At this, the kinsman-redeemer said, "Then I cannot redeem it because I might endanger my own estate. You redeem it yourself. I cannot do it." (Now in earlier times in Israel, for the redemption and transfer of property to become final, one party took off his sandal and gave it to the other. This was the method of legalizing transactions in Israel.) So the kinsman-redeemer said to Boaz, "Buy it yourself." And he removed his sandal.

Then Boaz announced to the elders and to all the people, "Today you are witnesses that I have bought from Naomi all the property of Elimelech, Kilion and Mahlon. I have acquired Ruth the Moabitess, Mahlon's widow as my wife, in order to maintain the name of the dead with his property, so that his name will not disappear from among his family or from the town records. Today you are my witnesses!"

Then the elders and all those at the gate said, "We are witnesses. May the Lord make the woman who is coming into your home like Rachel and Leah, who together built up the house of Israel. May you have standing in Ephrathah and be famous in Bethlehem. Through the offspring the Lord gives you by this young woman, may your family be like that of Perez, whom Tamar bore to Judah."

So Boaz took Ruth and she became his wife. Then he went to her, and the Lord enabled her to conceive, and she gave birth to a son. The women said to Naomi; "Praise be to the Lord, who this day has not left you without a kinsman-redeemer. May he become famous throughout Israel! He will renew your life and sustain you in your old age. For your daughter-in-law, who loves you and who is better to you than seven sons, has given him birth."

Then Naomi took the child, laid him in her lap and cared for him. The women living there said; "Naomi has a son." And they named him Obed. He was the father of Jesse, the father of David.

This, then, is the family line of Perez; Perez was the father of Hezron

Hezron the father of Ram,

Ram the father of Amminadab,

Amminadab the father of Nahshon,

Nahshon the father of Salmon,

Salmon the father of Boaz,

Boaz the father of Obed,

Obed the father of Jesse,

And Jesse the father of David.

"Praise be to the Lord who this day has not left you without a Kinsman Redeemer". My friend, they may as well have been screaming those words to us. Do you know that because of the sacrifice of Ruth, the spiritual leadership of Naomi, and the Obedience of Boaz, we have a Kinsman Redeemer in Jesus Christ. That little baby Obed, was David's grandfather. And, out of the house of David came Jesus.

We never know what our living and loving on purpose will one day conceive, but God does. This leads me to my last point; In order to live and love on purpose we need to take Godly risks and trust God with the outcome.

Living and loving on purpose is risky. It's plain risky. Let's look at the kinsman- redeemer who was actually first in line to redeem Ruth. He was all in at first, until he noticed there was risk involved. Go to verse Ruth 4:6; "At this, the kinsman-redeemer said; "Then I cannot redeem it because I might endanger my own estate. You redeem it yourself, I cannot do it".

This man (who wasn't even given a name, and I don't think that was a coincidence) had no lasting significance in God's plan. It was almost as if God said: "I don't care, just call him kinsman-redeemer. Even the prostitutes, tax collectors, murderers, and such, were allowed to be named in the bible, perhaps because they actually had some positive impacts on the kingdom. This man cared more about his property and what was at risk for him financially, than he cared about loving God and loving his neighbor. Therefore he wasn't given a name. He was unable to get past his fear of endangering his estate. Because of his self-centeredness and greed he missed out on being named in history as a man that shared in the lineage of Jesus.

Living and loving on purpose requires Godly risk and trusting God with the outcome. Boaz was ready to take some risks at redeeming Ruth. Ruth was ready to take some risks at putting herself out there hoping to be accepted by Boaz; Naomi took some risks at considering Ruth to be her daughter and taking the responsibility of becoming her spiritual authority.

How about us friend? What kind of Godly risks are you committed to take to see God's will revealed in your life?

How many children are in need of lasting families in our foster care system, but we can't risk having them around our children. After all, do we know what they have been exposed to?

How many single moms are trying to be both mom and dad to our future generation, when so many of us could step up and welcome them to our house on holidays or for Sunday dinners, but we can't risk having to entertain them, when it is just easier to include just our family?

How many elderly people are sitting in nursing homes day after day with no one to visit them; because we can't risk letting ourselves get too attached and then have to say good bye when they go home to see the Lord?

How many children are in public schools waiting for other Godly influences to reach out and talk to them about Jesus? But we can't risk those unsaved kids around ours. So we better put them in private school or homeschool them?

How many times do you hear the Holy Spirit screaming at you to let it go and forgive when you are arguing with your husband but we can't risk looking weak and being labeled the one that was wrong in the situation?

My friend, living and loving on purpose requires taking Godly risks and trusting God with the outcomes.

God showed me the other night at dinner with my sisters that in order for me to live in that sweet spot with Him, as I want to; I am going to have to take some Godly risks and trust Him with the outcome. Once a year when my sisters visit from NY, we all go out for a girl's night out, which is usually dinner and a movie. My mom raised 6 daughters and a son, so needless to say, there was never a dull moment growing up.

Well, my sister Char who was in a car accident 10 years ago is a paraplegic. During all of her healing, they had to do a tracheotomy, so she still has some scar tissue from the procedure. This causes her to choke very easily. Well, it just so happens that three of the times that Char has been desperately choking, I have been with her, and had to do the Heimlich maneuver on her. The other night was the third time.

I was at the total other end of the table with five other ladies in between us. I watched a couple of my sisters trying to pat her on the back, thinking that she would just cough it up. Well, I waited just as long as my little flesh could handle and I shoved them out of the way and went to town helping her.

This is not the only time I have pushed people out of the way when I saw someone choking. I have also shoved a complete stranger off of his wife at Disney world when she was choking on popcorn, and I saw him doing the Heimlich wrong. That day afterwards; my in-laws kept saying; "Mo, he probably thought you were a nurse or doctor or some kind of trained professional the way you took control"

I thought; *nope not even a candy striper ever-control freak... maybe?*

I've Heimliched my niece in a softball dugout, as she was choking on hard candy. I am sure countless times I have yanked my babies out of the high chairs, when they were choking; but officially in public, this was number 5!

Not because I even remember my training from the babysitting class I took at 15 years old, when I was CPR certified; but because truly, somewhere deep down in my spirit, where only Jesus lives, I believe that when I fight on the side of love, peace, patience, kindness, gentleness, faithfulness and self – control; God will have my back!

Let's look at Psalm 91; we are going to read this one together. Please read this entire Psalm out loud so that the truths can do into your heart. We need to get a holy confidence among God's people and an assurance that God's Word is completely true; especially the parts about not being afraid and trusting God to fight for us.

Psalm 91

Whoever dwells in the shelter of the Most High
will rest in the shadow of the Almighty.[a]
2 I will say of the LORD, "He is my refuge and my fortress,
my God, in whom I trust."

3 Surely he will save you
from the fowler's snare
and from the deadly pestilence.
4 He will cover you with his feathers,
and under his wings you will find refuge;
his faithfulness will be your shield and rampart.
5 You will not fear the terror of night,
nor the arrow that flies by day,
6 nor the pestilence that stalks in the darkness,
nor the plague that destroys at midday.
7 A thousand may fall at your side,
ten thousand at your right hand,
but it will not come near you.
8 You will only observe with your eyes
and see the punishment of the wicked.

9 If you say, "The LORD is my refuge,"
and you make the Most High your dwelling,
10 no harm will overtake you,
no disaster will come near your tent.

[11] For he will command his angels concerning you
to guard you in all your ways;
[12] they will lift you up in their hands,
so that you will not strike your foot against a stone.
[13] You will tread on the lion and the cobra;
you will trample the great lion and the serpent.

[14] "Because he[b] loves me," says the LORD, "I will rescue him;
I will protect him, for he acknowledges my name.
[15] He will call on me, and I will answer him;
I will be with him in trouble,
I will deliver him and honor him.
[16] With long life I will satisfy him
and show him my salvation."

I can just feel Satan squirming in his seat as God's Word about His protection, His deliverance and His promises are read out loud like this. My friend; if we are willing to dwell in the shelter of The Most High; (dwell means stay) we can take some Godly risks for the Kingdom, and watch God move.

The book of Ruth is not just a story my friend. It is our history. It is the family tree and ancestry of our Kinsman Redeemer Jesus.

The book of Ruth shows us how to live and love on purpose. As God's ambassadors, we must be committed, we must go the extra mile, we must be obedient, and we must take some Godly risks and trust God with the outcome.

It's all about decisions. Today will you make a decision to live and love on purpose?

Let's study a little about taking Godly risks and trusting God with the outcome:

- I want to encourage you to memorize Psalm 91 and pray it daily over your family, your home and your loved ones. You will never regret arming yourself with the amazing promises written in this Psalm.

Let's Pray:
Heavenly Father, we come to you in your precious Son Jesus' name and we say thank you. Thank you for not leaving us without a Kinsman-Redeemer. Thank you that Jesus will never leave us, nor forsake us. We are Unforsaken! Thank you that your Word in the Book of Ruth teaches us to live and love on purpose. We want to live purposeful lives. We love you and we praise you in Jesus' name, Amen.

- Journal a prayer to God thanking Him for what you learned by reading the entire book of Ruth: Great job by the way!

Harvest Time

Posted on August 30, 2012 by momydlo www.wordpress.com

With fall approaching, I get an excited anticipation of things to come. Fall means cooler days to play some catch out back, decorating the front porch with pumpkins and mums, and Friday night football games.

But more than any of these things, I am excited about harvest time in the Kingdom of God. When we plant seeds of faith into people's lives, seeds of love, compassion, or kindness, our God takes these seeds; and He brings the harvest.

We can't make things grow, only God can. However, God needs farmers that will be willing to do the planting, watering, and weeding. God needs us to be His hired hands and feet in HIS garden.

Think about a pumpkin, when you carve a pumpkin that is fully grown and open it up, you see thousands of seeds inside just waiting to be planted. Every time there is a harvest, there are more seeds to be planted.

That is what it is like to be a Christian. Somebody sowed some seeds to lead you to the One who can grow you up. Then, God expects us to sow seeds of our own. An important note is that while He is cultivating those seeds, He doesn't neglect the fruit in our lives. It just seems to get softer and sweeter as we grow.

Let's Study A Little About Harvest Time:

Read the following scriptures

- Matthew 9:35-38

- 2 Corinthians 9:6-11

- Galatians 6:7-10

In the book of Ruth, we learned that sowing seeds of commitment, going the extra mile, obedience and taking Godly risks and trusting God all reap a good harvest.

In your walk with Christ, where have you been sowing good seed? Where have you been scattering seeds that seem to just keep floating away in the wind?

- Journal a prayer to God asking Him to show you good soil to sow into:

Room By Room

Posted on February 11, 2013 by momydlo www.wordpress.com

Do you ever get overwhelmed when it is time to clean the house? Sometimes I have to really get myself prayed up to get started on the house. Today I was running through the house making beds and picking up morning laundry, when I thought to myself, cleaning this house is so much easier if I focus on one room at a time.

I don't know if you have a certain method as to how you clean your house; but being the creature of habit that I am, I do. I usually start in the back and work forward. Then after I finish picking up a room, I move to the next. Sometimes when I am a little distracted, I find myself bouncing around between rooms, making a bed, then maybe loading the dishwasher, starting the vacuum then doing another bed. I realized I waste more time cleaning that way, and that lack of concentration on one area, can make me feel overwhelmed and want to quit. So, I really try to focus on one room at a time.

Why do I share this rather boring Mo fact with you? Well, just like many things during the day, I think God reveals His heart to us through simple everyday tasks and events. Today I thought to myself, *this is how God cleans us up*. He starts on one stronghold that the enemy has tried to bind us to; He frees us as we submit to His leading; then He moves on. He then finds another habit or sin that we have clung to as born-again believers and He convicts us of it, convinces us to repent of it, then He moves on. He then finds an area in which maybe we are in need of some healing, and He encourages us in His Word to release our faith in that area. When He heals us He moves on.

The Grace Race

Yes, God is a God of order. He doesn't just change us immediately into His image the second we become born again. He gives us His righteousness, and then He puts on His cleaning gloves to get to work. You see God is smart enough to know that we are all tangled up like a strand of Christmas lights just waiting to be unraveled; and the best way to make the mixed up areas in our lives straight is to begin to pull them out one chord at a time!

Perhaps some of you may take this as cleaning advice. If so, I hope it is a blessing. But, believe me; I'm not handing out laundry advice. I think I am missing an enzyme where the love of laundry gene is concerned. I've turned more tighty -whities into pink than I care to admit to. However, keeping a neat house, I will say, regarding that one, I feel confident handing out some advice.

My true prayer is that you take the Spiritual advice I have in here for you and stand with me as we allow God to work on us one day at a time, one sin at a time, one habit and stronghold at a time. Then, someday we can stand before Him just thankful that we were obedient to His cleaning.

Let's Study A Little About Obedience:

Ruth understood obedience. Let's read about our friend Jonah who needed a little bit more help understanding obedience.

- Read the Book of Jonah. Chapters 1-4

- What were the consequences of Jonah's initial disobedience?

- Do you think God will get His way in your life whether you fight Him or not?

- Journal a prayer to God asking Him to help you choose obedience to His cleansing process.

Trust and Obey All That's Real is Today!

Posted on March 29, 2013 by momydlo www.wordpress.com

I had to really think to myself; have you titled a different blog "trust and obey"? I realized it is kind of becoming my motto and stance where my walk with The Lord is concerned. He showed me this little message well over a year ago, and He has been driving the point home ever since. Trust and obey. All that's real is today!

Why does God want us to just trust Him day by day? Well, speaking from embarrassing experience, it's probably because we can't handle the future, and we struggle to let go of the past. Our only peace comes when we walk day by day with Him as our guide. This morning I woke up at 5:00 am after speaking yesterday at an event and staying up until well over midnight. You would think that my body would be so tired that I would have just slept through God's nudge, but I can't stand to miss out when He has something for me, so I just put on the coffee and my robe and I sat quietly.

With this new endeavor of travelling, speaking and writing books for women, helping them to renew their minds, my natural inclination to buck against change has been kicked into high gear lately. I have had to fight fears of hearing Him wrong and sharing the wrong material, opposition from other teachers who may not appreciate my transparency, and anxiety of God providing for our financial needs with me out of the everyday workforce. Blah, blah, blah, I just hear the lies from the enemy, and I fight it with prayer and confessing God's Word.

God has been restraining my desire to look too far into the future by encouraging me to be like Abraham in the bible. He just went when God told him to go, not even knowing where he was going. God said; Go and Abraham went! Since God is the same yesterday, today and tomorrow, He seems to be using the same technique with me. And, believe me, it has been nerve wracking, but EXCITING!

He is testing my true belief in the fact that when I say; "I AM UNFORSAKEN" I truly know it! He is showing me one day out, where to go, what to say, who to reach, and what to write. My friend, this is a whole new life for me, and guess what? I FEEL FREE! I have this deep trust in my heart that no matter where He leads me; He is there! That's enough for me.

This morning my devotional I read was pretty much spot on with what I have been feeling; the first few words said; "Stop trying to work things out before their times have come". Oh, I am so guilty of that. I have a 3 point plan on how to handle whatever circumstance life may ever throw at me in the natural. That my friend, is called; "A CONTROL FREAK". And to that lifestyle, God warns me to stop!

After I read that devotional, my next one was of course, about blind faith. Then the scripture He led me to during my bible reading time was; Isaiah 42:16. I would like to share this with all of my fellow worriers, planners and control freaks. This one is for us.
"I will lead the blind by ways they have not known, along unfamiliar paths I will guide them; I will turn the darkness into light before them and make the rough places smooth. These are the things I will do. I will not forsake them."

Sweet friend of mine; YOU ARE UNFORSAKEN! He desires that we let Him lead. He goes before us. He chooses to only light the path immediately in front of us. God doesn't use high beams. Trust and obey. All that's real is today!

Let's Study A Little About Trusting and Obeying:

Ruth understood how to trust God and obey Him each day. What a blessing to have studied under her teaching.

Read the following scriptures:

- Proverbs 3:5-6

- Romans 9:30-33

- Journal a prayer to God thanking Him that when you trust in Him, you will never be put to shame:

3.

Fight The Good Fight of Faith

1 Timothy 6:12; "Fight the good fight of the faith. Take hold of the eternal life to which you were called when you made your good confession in the presence of many witnesses."

I love this passage. First of all, we need to understand that this is the apostle Paul encouraging his disciple Timothy. He had just talked to Timothy about not being swayed by the love of money. He was explaining contentment to him, not saying that money is evil, but the love of money. He is truly trying to keep him protected from that.

The verse before he was talking about fighting the good fight, he says; *"But, you, man of God, flee from all of this, and pursue righteousness, godliness, faith, love, endurance and gentleness."* He's trying to teach him to watch how he starts feeling about money, and pursue righteousness at the same time. Now, this is quite obviously a decision that Timothy will have to make. He will have to flee from one, and pursue another and this will take a bit of fighting.

This fighting we are familiar with aren't we my friend? Paul was only talking about the love of money here, but we as modern day believers have many other things that our flesh (our sin nature) will desire that is contrary to what the Spirit will desire, and we will have to flee from the first and pursue the things of the Spirit.

Does this mean we will have to literally run? Maybe from some things. It depends on what your flesh may be vying for that is contrary to the Spirit. If you have a drinking problem and you are walking by a bar and you feel your flesh tempting you to walk in, I'm telling you to run. Run like you are being chased! If it's those Oreos that are tempting you and you are trying to do a gluten free diet. I'm telling you to run away from that pantry and towards the blueberries. I am serious. Sometimes we have to get a little radical to live a holy life that is pleasing to The Lord.

Paul tells Timothy to take hold of the eternal life to which he was called when he made his good confession. Dear friend, what is that good confession? We all have to make this confession if we want to see Jesus face to face someday and walk into the gates of Heaven when we die. That confession is Jesus is Lord. That is the good confession that Paul is talking about. Confessing and making Jesus Lord of our life, changes everything for us, starting with our salvation, our names being written in the Lambs book of life and then it should begin to change how we live while we are here.

Taking hold of the eternal life to which we were called involves some fighting. We will have to fight our flesh, we will have to fight temptation from the enemy, and we will have to fight living like the world. Did you recognize that something happened when you became a Christian? Did you slowly begin to recognize that certain things that you did before you were walking with Jesus didn't bother your conscience? But, now, you do them, and you get that nudging and conviction in your belly, kind of like dinner just didn't settle right? I know this proved true with me.

I used to love the soap opera; "The Guiding Light." I would rush home from high school, to find out what was going on in Springfield, and with Beth and Phillip. After I was saved I began going to a bible study at a friend's house. This first bible study group gave me my very own bible, they taught me my first scriptures to memorize to combat anxiety and these women were amazing to me. Well, the leader of the group, Gretchen was asking us to pray for her to stop watching "Days of Our Lives." I couldn't understand why. I thought; *what is wrong with soap operas? I'm never going to stop watching Guiding light? I mean, what would I do at 3pm? That's naptime, that's me time.*

After I had been a Christian a while, and I was watching soaps one day, and I started feeling a little icky. I remember thinking; *"Oh, no Gretchen, you're not praying this on me"*. But, it wasn't Gretchen my friends. I was reading the Word in the morning, and what I was watching on the show, wasn't lining up with what I was trying to live like, and God convicted me. That icky feeling is conviction. It is God's way of growing us up. Puberty, makes us feel pretty icky, but that awkwardness is what God uses to make us mature into adulthood.

Paul is in essence saying to Timothy; *"You made your public good confession. Now, it's time to take hold of what God saved you for, start living a life worthy of the call."*

Let's Study a Little About Our Good Confession:

Read the following scriptures:

- Romans 10: 8-10

- 2 Corinthians 9: 13-15

- Philippians 2: 9-11

Have you made your good confession that Jesus is Lord? I can promise you that you do not want to wait. Your eternal salvation relies on you making Jesus Lord of your life. There truly is no other name in Heaven or on earth by which men can be saved. John 14:4: "Jesus answered, 'I am the way and the truth and the life. No one comes to the Father except through me.'" There is nothing more to be said here except; JESUS IS LORD!

- Journal a prayer to God thanking Him for sending His Son Jesus Christ to die on the cross to forgive you for your sins, for raising Him three days later, and for allowing you to have a personal relationship with a very real and living God:

3.
Fight The Good Fight of Faith

Fighting the good fight of faith is not easy is it friend? Do you know Christians are three part beings… a Spirit, a soul, and a body. Our Spirit belongs to the devil until it belongs to Jesus when we make Him Lord. When we do that, our Sprit becomes just like Jesus because it is The Holy Spirit. Our soul makes up our mind, emotions and intellect and our bodies are designed to follow the five senses. After we are born again, though our Spirit becomes changed immediately our soul and our bodies only know what they have always known. We have to fight the good fight of faith to get our souls and our bodies to line up with our Spirit.

We do this by renewing our minds daily in the Word of God and allowing the Holy Spirit and the supernatural power of the Bible to change us. This takes time.   It takes time, effort and sacrifice. But, becoming all that God has called you to be is worth it!

Every battle requires a battleground. And, where the area of Spiritual warfare is concerned, the battle is mostly in the mind. Proverbs 23:7 says; "As a man thinketh so in his heart, so is he". Our stinkin thinkin, gets us into trouble my friends. Poor thinking is the first step into sinning. We don't just sin. It starts with a thought. But, when our thinking is lined up with what God thinks, which is everything written in The Word of God, we have victory.

Jesus says; "Cast all of your cares on me, for I care for you." The Devil attacks your thinking with; Control this! If you don't worry about it; who will?

Jesus says; "Peace be with you." The Devil attacks your thinking with; Figure this out! There's got to be an answer to this. Don't stop till you think it to death.

Jesus says; "Do not worry about tomorrow; tomorrow has enough worries of it's own." The Devil attacks your thinking with; "what if this happens, what will you do? Where will you go? How can you fix it?

Jesus says; "Your sins are forgiven, go now, and leave your life of sin." The Devil attacks your mind with; "How in the world could you have done that? Your past is going to catch up with you, they are going to figure out how messed up you are. You must not even be saved."

Here's the truth. Every word, every promise and every scripture in this bible is truth. If you are thinking something that is opposite of what you have studied in the bible, you are under the attack of the enemy, and you must flee. You must run from the fiery darts of the enemy, and towards the loving arms of our Savior and rest in the peace of the Word of God. We must learn to do this every day, because the fight goes on, whether we are armed and prepared or not.

How do we arm ourselves? I promise you, I will never stop telling you in everything I write and teach, arm yourself from the attack of the enemy by daily renewing your mind in the Word of God and with prayer. We cannot just read the word, or just pray. You fight the devil with a combination of praying and studying the Word every day. You will also have to learn how to say the word out loud at the enemy.

The Word says; *"Faith comes by hearing, and hearing by the Word of God".* We must say truths out loud to ourselves so it goes out our mouths, in our ears, and then can penetrate your heart. Our hearts are obstinent. Our heart wants what it always has gotten before because it is selfish. Remember, our emotions and our intellect weren't changed at the moment of our good confession, only our Spirit was. The Word spoken out loud over our own lives is what changes our souls and brings our bodies into submission.

In Galatians 5:16 Paul says; *"So I say, live by the Spirit and you will not gratify the desires of the sinful nature. For the sinful nature desires what is contrary to the Spirit and the Spirit what is contrary to the sinful nature. They are in conflict with each other."* Dear friend, your own mind and body will fight against what God is trying to do in your Spirit. You have to crucify your old flesh and die to that old self every day, so that you can live the life God has desired for you to live.

Let's study a little about our Spirit, Soul and Body.

Read the following scriptures:

- 1 Thessalonians 5:23

- Matthew 10:28

- James 2:26

- Ecclesiastes 12:7

- Hebrews 4:12

God is not saving your victory for when you get to Heaven. God wants you to be successful, and victorious here, living as a Christian. Allow The Word of God to penetrate your heart daily as you renew your mind to the truths in God's Word.

- Journal a prayer to God asking Him to help you to train your soul and your body to submit to His Spirit living inside of you.

3.
Fight The Good Fight of Faith

"Finally, be strong in the Lord and in His mighty power. Put on the armor of God so that you can take your stand against the devil's schemes. For our struggle is not against flesh and blood, but against the rulers, against the authorities against the powers of this dark world and against the Spiritual forces of evil in Heavenly realms. Therefore, put on the full armor of God so that when the day of evil comes, you may be able to stand your ground, and after you have done everything, to stand. Stand firm then with the belt of truth buckled around your waste, with the breastplate of righteousness in place, and with your feet fitted with the readiness that comes from the gospel of peace. In addition to all of this, take up the shield of faith with which you can extinguish all of the flaming arrows of the evil one. Take the helmet of salvation and the sword of the Spirit, which is The Word of God". And, pray in the Spirit on all occasions with all kinds of prayers and requests."

I love this truth in Ephesians but I especially love how Paul basically says; "oh, and pray all of the time and everywhere."

Do you think you can get away without praying my friend? Oh, you can give it a try and see how you do. I can't! I pray all day, about everything. I pray little prayers, big prayers, driving in the car prayers, in my kitchen cooking prayers, walking on the road prayers, in my bible study chair prayers, and on my face with my dog looking at me like I am dead prayers.

Prayer is huge. I think that is why Paul lists it last in this armor of God scenario. It's that old adage that you usually remember the first things said and the last things said.

He does that in this passage. He starts out with; *"Be strong in the Lord"'* and he ends it with; *"pray in the Spirit on all occasions with all kinds of prayers."* Why? Because in order to win, we have a secret weapon…God. He is our ringer. He is our starting lineup in the game. He is our MVP and our go-to player.

Apart from God: What does the word say we can do? NOTHING! We can do nothing, without Him. But we all know what the awesome Tim Tebow (a football player for The University of Florida) always had face painted on his face during games: *Philippians 4:13 says; "I can do all things through Christ who gives me strength."*

We fight the enemy with The Word, and with the Lord. With that combination, we win!

We fight the enemy by staying in the moment. Remember the motto that I taught you in chapter 1: *Trust and obey all that's real is today?* You see, we get hung up usually in our minds over two things; guilt of the past, and fear of the future. Can you attest to that?

We feel guilty about past sins that most likely we have already repented for and God has truly already forgiven and forgotten. Or, we worry about our futures not turning out exactly as a fairy tale would depict a happily ever after. Very seldom are the events of that very moment where we struggle. You know why? Because God's grace covers what is going on in the present.

God is alive and active working in our present circumstances. He is finished with the past, and He knows we can't handle knowing what is to happen in the future. When we are in the moment and we are under God's grace then we are free. Yes, our battle in the mind and is usually focused on the past or the future.

I'm thankful that God showed me Trust and Obey, all that's real, is today.

We first have to fight the guilt of our past. Our past is what we run from, where we messed up, where we spoke something we shouldn't have, done something wrong, and made a wrong choice. Since we cannot create a time machine and go back to change and undo what we have already done, repentance and forgiveness are the keys.

Jesus paid the penalty on the cross. His blood was shed and His life was taken so that we could receive the forgiveness that God desires us to receive by grace through faith, with nothing that we could possibly do to deserve it. Yet, we still trample that sacrifice underfoot by not forgiving ourselves for past mistakes and sins.

The other night I couldn't sleep. It was four am and I woke up from a nightmare that felt much too real. It was one of my past failures coming back to haunt me. Sins that I had repented for, been forgiven for by God, and yet still was allowing the enemy to torment me with through guilt and condemnation.

The devil was using his usual, *"Oh, you just wait till they find out the real you"* technique with me. *"You can't possibly be used by God."* *"You are a mess. A Hypocrite".*

What I was saying to God by allowing the devil to tell me these lies, and not just roll over and go back to bed was; *"your sacrifice wasn't enough."* *"your beatings weren't enough"* *"Your blood wasn't enough".* *I have to still punish myself."* That's what we are doing my friend when we fail to let God's forgiveness cover us, and put the past to death once and for all.

That morning I felt The Holy Spirit nudge me and proclaim that I have to forgive myself and let go of the past, because Jesus has already paid the price and there is no sacrifice needed.

His Word says in Proverbs 19:9: *"A false witness will not go unpunished and he who pours out lies will perish."* Dear friend, when I say that I believe in my heart that Jesus has paid the price for my sins on Calvary yet I still allow the enemy to get me feeling guilty and condemned; I am a false witness against myself.

When the gospel which means: *news almost too good to be true* tells me that I am forgiven, and I still feel guilty, I am a false witness against myself. I am forgiven because of what Jesus did. I have to stand strong in that forgiveness and not allow the enemy to put me back on the witness stand against myself. He is the accuser of the brethren, and that devil lives to torment us about our past. We have to fight him by standing on the truth.

The Word says; *"I set before you, life and death, choose life."* My friend, where the guilt of our past or the fear of the future concerned, there are two choices you can make. You can run into the open arms of Jesus who is ready to wrap you in His robe of righteousness and wash you clean by His blood or you can step into the wrong line of an accuser standing there with a whip in his hands ready to beat you silly with guilt and condemnation.

We have all lined up in the wrong lines before… amen? But, just like our computers needed a reboot to work right sometimes, so do we, friend. We need to unplug from the lies, rest in God's presence, and then plug back into the Word so that we can move ahead with The Lord.

God's grace is in the present. He's finished with our past. He's placed it at the bottom of the ocean.

Let's Study A Little About God's Forgiveness:

Read the following scriptures:

- Romans 8:1

- Hebrews 8:12

- Hebrews 10:17-18

- 1 John 1:9

Today, will you allow Jesus to truly forgive you for your past so that you can become all that He has designed you to be?

- Journal a prayer to God asking Him to forgive you for your sins, and help you to forgive yourself, so that you can receive your freedom in Christ.

3.

Fighting The Good Fight of Faith

We still have to fight another area in which the devil wants to get us stuck; fear of the future.

Here is the most common question that the ugly devil wants you pondering; *"what if, what if, what if? "What if something happens to my kids? What if my husband leaves? What if this tumor is cancerous? What if we lose the house? What if I mess up? What if this is it? What if what if, what if?*

I know you may have heard the word fear taken apart letter by letter spelling FEAR; False Evidence Appearing Real.

Jesus knew we were going to struggle with worrying about the future; that is why he said; *"Do not worry about tomorrow. For tomorrow will have enough worries of it's own. Who of you from worrying, can add a single hour to his life?"* God wants to teach us that tomorrow is going to have problems, you just can't focus on them. First of all, you can't fix them because you don't even know what they are going to be. You can't tell the future because God knew we couldn't handle that kind of power. We would become control crazy, trying to avoid any pain, struggles and hardships. As bad as this sounds; God allows some trials to happen to us, because it is for our own good, and it grows us up. If we try to control these events, God can't grow us into mature Christians.

Jesus didn't even let the disciples know too far in advance when His time to die was coming. He didn't tell them until it was the night of the last supper. They truly didn't know it was coming that soon, because Jesus knew they couldn't handle it. They wouldn't understand it, and they weren't going to change it whether they knew or not.

God is a God of today. He doesn't want us fearing tomorrow. His Word starts many phrases with *"Today…." "God's Word says; "today, if you hear His voice, do not harden your heart." "But encourage each other daily, as long as it is called today." "Give us today, our daily bread."* He teaches the disciples to pray for "today" in The Lord's prayer. God only gave the Israelites enough manna (or food) to feed them for that day, one day at a time. God wants us living one day at a time as well.

Fear of the future can lead to so many problems… mental, emotional and physical.

Fear of lack can cause us to be greedy and not give as God tells us to or cause us to hoard up things around us that can begin to strangle us with their own kind of torment.

Fear of loss can make us lose precious time with our loved ones that are here right now because we are worrying about them leaving us.

Fear of messing up can keep us from trying new things that God wants us to do such as creating new ministries, inventing new things, or serving in a new capacity.

Fear of change can keep us in our comfort zones never allowing us to experience the ultimate joy and happiness that God desires for us.

Fear of being alone can cause us to push away those that are closest to us by ignoring them and drowning in our own selfish thinking and obsessive thinking.

God desires that we live in the present, because the tormenting fear of loss that thinking about the future can bring robs our todays. We go to bed exhausted from days of trying to control everything around us to secure our tomorrows, and we when realize today is gone, we can't get it back. The Israelites were only given their daily bread, because if God gave them more than they needed, it would rot.

Fear of tomorrow robs us of our todays, damages our health and destroys our relationships. God loves us too much for that. He wants us to enjoy our every day. That is why He teaches us in His Word to live in the moment.

When God gave me; *Trust and Obey. All that's real is today*; I believe it is because today is all that we have any control over. The control is only; to trust and obey God.

Today He wants us to trust Him and obey Him and study our bibles. He wants us to trust Him and obey Him and spend time praying and seeking His will for our lives. Today, trust Him, obey Him and love our husbands and our kids. Today, trust Him, obey Him and serve in our ministry. Today, trust Him, obey Him and work hard at our jobs. Today, trust Him, obey Him and…go for walks, swing on swings, take bike rides, go for swims, hug our dogs, dance with our babies, watch our kids grow. .My friend, our peace, our joy, our abundance, our blessing and our lives are covered in His grace for today.

Let's Study A Little About Not Worrying About Tomorrow:

Read the following scriptures:

- Isaiah 41:10

- Psalm 55:22

- Matthew 6:25-34

- Luke 21:14

Will you today, make an effort to trust God, obey Him and only focus on today? I promise, your peace will amaze you.

Journal a prayer to God asking Him to help you stay in the moment:

Sesame Street

Posted on September 11, 2012 by momydlo www.wordpress.com

I was out staining my deck and I realized I didn't have enough stain to do the complete floor of the deck, so I mixed it with a little water to stretch it. Stain is much more forgiving than paint, so it turned out ok, but it could use another coat to protect it better. When I am out on my deck, I can't help but talk to God and praise Him for His many blessings in my life.

I just kept thinking of the old Sesame Street song; "One of these things doesn't belong here". They used to teach kids classification by putting four boxes on the screen, you would sing the song, and then figure out which item didn't belong with the others. Do you remember this one?

Anyways, I was thinking about the stain and the water that I was mixing. It really wasn't working because oil and water just doesn't go together. But, more than oil and water, I was thinking of biblical truths of things that just don't go together. Things like fear and faith. We cannot be in fear when we are in complete faith. We cannot be in sorrow when we focus on the joy of the Lord. We cannot be in anxiety when we are in prayer.

If you are struggling today with anxiety or fear or depression, try digging in to God's Word and meditating on truths about the opposite feelings… peace, faith, and joy. The Word is what heals us. We need to renew our mind to line up with truths. Our feelings lie to us. We need to stop bowing down to our feelings so much and bow down to the Prince of Peace.

The Grace Race

We need to remember some of the great lessons we learned from Sesame Street. Big Bird and Grover would be so proud of us!

Let's Study A Little about Faith:

Read the following scriptures:

- Matthew 17:14-20

- Matthew: 21:18-22

- Hebrews 11:1

I want to encourage you to today to practice faith, so that fear will disappear. You can't be in fear and in faith at the same time.

- Journal a prayer to God asking Him to grow your faith in Him.

The Washing of the Word

Posted on October 30, 2012 by momydlo www.wordpress.com

If you have ever had surgery of any kind, you know that it is very important to keep the incision area very clean to prevent any type of infection. I have been reminded of this lately, after just having some minor surgery. I am careful about washing my hands well before I clean and bandage the area, and I have been extra careful lately about germs.

As I was looking in the mirror today at my bandage, I was thinking about how the Jewish priests of Jesus' day would have to stand at what was called the laver before they entered the sanctuary. The brass of this basin would reveal their reflection so they could see where they needed to wash before they entered the Holy of Holies. Then they would clean themselves carefully to be as pure as they could be on entering.

I am so very grateful that Jesus chooses to live inside of us as a sanctuary for His Spirit, no matter how dirty it was when He entered. We were all filthy with sin, yet He cared enough to lay down His life to make us clean enough to enter Heaven someday.

But, daily we still need to bath. I'm not just talking about a physical cleansing for our bodies. I am talking about a Spiritual bathing of our hearts as the Sanctuary of the Holy Spirit. In Ephesians 5: 26 it reads: "to make her holy, cleansing her by the washing with water through the Word and to present her to himself as a radiant church, without stain or wrinkle or any other blemish, but holy and blameless".

I know my physical body is prone to wrinkles, blemishes, and stains and if I did not care for it daily, it would be covered with such. How much more does God want us to care for the Spirit that was entrusted to us on the day we made Him Lord? We need to daily renew our minds in the Word of God, so that when the ugliness of unnecessary guilt comes our way, we can wash it away with truth and when the vileness of fear or anxiety shows up we can be cleansed from it by The Word; or when the smell of temptations and sin start stinking up our life again, we can bath in the truths of God's testimony.

Yes, I love my daily washing of the Word. Dive in! The water is always perfect!

Let's Study a Little About Daily Renewing our Minds:

Read the following scriptures:

- Romans 12:1-2

- 2 Corinthians 4:16-18

- Titus 3: 3-7

I want to encourage you today to renew your mind, will and emotions to line up with the many beautiful truths in God's Word.

- Journal a prayer to God asking Him to wash you today with the living water of The Word:

Freedom

Posted on June 10, 2013 by momydlo www.wordpress.com

"It is for freedom that Christ has set us free. Stand firm, then, and do not let yourselves be burdened again by a yoke of slavery." Galatians 5:1. Our family went on a little weekend trip to the beach, and nothing makes me feel closer to God than looking out at the ocean with nothing but the horizon in sight. I was sitting in my chair watching Eli (my youngest) jump waves, punch waves, toss his ball into the waves and retrieve it himself. He was enjoying God's playground and I felt like a kid again just watching him.

You see, Eli is a child, and he sees life from faith to faith to faith. He puts his faith in the fact that there will be food in the fridge to feed him each day. He puts his faith in the fact that he will have clean clothes to get dressed with each day. He puts his faith in the fact that the sun will come out from behind the clouds so he can take a dip in the pool. Eli trusts that his needs are taken care of, and he is left simply to enjoy life.

That is exactly how God desires us to live. He wants us to experience the freedom that He died for. He doesn't want us worrying everyday about possible disasters are around every corner, or getting caught up in our mistakes of yesterday. He simply wants us to be free. Free to live, free to love, and free to share His love and grace with others.

We could all take a few lessons from Eli. Every day I look at him and praise God that he is a fun-magnet. His favorite foods are Funyons and Fun-dip, he cannon- balls every time he jumps in any pool, and he skips into the store when we are running errands. My husband always says; "you can't skip, unless you are happy." Yes, we could all take some lessons from Eli.

It is God's will that we have freedom and joy. He wanted it for us so badly, he sacrificed His son.

Let's Study A Little About Freedom In Christ:

Read the following scriptures:

- John 8:31-32

- Acts 13:38-39

- Romans 8: 1-4

Stand firm today. Do not let that enemy burden you with any yoke of slavery. You are free in Christ.

- Journal a prayer to God asking Him to help you remember that you are free indeed:

4.
Insecurity

Insecurity is that ugly little voice that we have grown so accustomed to that travels with us in our suitcases of life whispering words that make us feel unsteady, uncertain, unsure of ourselves, unguarded and unprotected; plenty of "uns" right?

Usually "uns" aren't something that we like, so if we can get rid of the "uns" we can begin to feel steady, certain, sure of ourselves, guarded and protected. That seems like it will work, but it may be easier said than done right?

Insecurity is something that we can beat, but it will be with the same prescription that I have given you book after book, blog after blog, message after message…we have to renew our minds in The Word of God.

We have to stop conforming to the patterns of this world and be transformed by the renewing of our minds so that we can test and approve what is God's perfect will for our lives…His good and perfect will for our lives.

God's Word is where we go for our help. Let's go there right now.

I want to introduce to you two men in the bible. The first man, I am going to crown The King of Insecurity actually was a king. He was the first king for the Israelites.

Israel was ruled by judges for years until they demanded from God a king. They wanted to be like other nations that had kings, God granted them their heart's desire, but of course, what we think we want isn't always what we need. God allowed them their freedom to choose and so God sent Saul.

King Saul was anointed as king by the prophet Samuel. Samuel was a God fearing judge, and when Saul took over as king, Israel went from being a theocracy (which means a country led by God) to a monarchy (one led by a king).

In the book of 1 Samuel, we meet Saul for the first time. Samuel had anointed him and it was time for Samuel to introduce him to the Israelites as their king. The following scripture represents Israel's first glimpse of their king. 1

Samuel 10:20; *"When Samuel brought all the tribes of Israel near, the tribe of Benjamin was chosen. Then he brought forward the tribe of Benjamin clan by clan, and Matri's clan was chosen. Finally Saul son of Kish was chosen. But when they looked for him, he was not to be found. So they inquired further of The Lord. "Has the man come here yet?" And The Lord said; "Yes, he has hidden himself among the baggage."*

Well, there you have it; *"he has hidden himself among the baggage."* Well, praise the Lord, here is our brave and noble new king, hidden in the Samsonite carryons. Not, the grand entrance we all would expect from our new king. Here's the thing; I'm not one of those people that follow the royal family in England, but I have seen *Princess Diaries*. I saw her coronation and even she looked a little more confident than that. After all, she wasn't hiding in a bunch of luggage.

Saul's insecurity made him hide from what was his God given destiny in life. And, sometimes don't we do the same?
Insecurity is one of those ugly relatives of fear. Why do we hide from our future dreams and plans that God has mapped out for us? Fear! Fear of not measuring up; fear of messing up; fear of falling on our face and letting people see that we are not perfect; fear of ending up alone; fear of people... you name it.

Insecurity made Saul hide, and it does the same for us. We hide behind masks that we create to cover our nakedness just as Adam and Eve did with loin cloths they made when they realized they were naked. Because they felt shame, they hid from God.

Oh, we hide in our comfort zones; we hide in our comfortable places that require no risk, or not trusting God because we feel safe there. We don't have to face those "what ifs" if we just hide behind the baggage that we have stacked around us.

Throughout my time in ministry I have met real people who have been abused and hurt so intensely in their past that they have created true physical barriers around themselves to stay safe.

I have met hoarders who have stockpiled stuff around them so deeply in their homes so that they don't have to face looking out windows to the outside world, or risk others seeing in to theirs.

I have met obese people who have eaten enormous amounts of food to build a barrier around themselves so that people will not look at them in a wrong or sexual way, because someone or some people have abused them in the past.

I have met battered women who will not lift their heads up to look you in the eyes, because they have been shamed so badly by someone who stole their strength to see the beauty all around them.

Yes, insecurity makes us hide in our baggage.

Let's Study About Stepping Out Of Our Comfort Zones:

Read the following scriptures:

- Joshua 1:9

- 2 Timothy 1:7

- James 1:22

- John 15:16

- Journal a Prayer to God asking Him to help you to take a step of faith with Him:

4.

Insecurity

1 Samuel 9:2 The Word says that Saul was *"an impressive young man without equal among the Israelites. He was a head taller than all of the others."*

Yes he was hiding in baggage, but he was tall. I just picture Will Ferrell in the movie Elf when he is sitting in Elf class, bursting out of his desk. The truth is, Saul was tall, dark and handsome. Wouldn't you think he would be secure in his new position as king? Seriously, isn't that how we think?

We look at women who are well put together with a beautiful figure, fancy clothes, nails, hair, you name it... We assume that they must never suffer with insecurity right? Wrong! Let me tell you, some of the most insecure women that I have met have worn the homecoming crown, cheered for the Varsity football team, and been class President all four years. I should know, I was that person.

Nothing will make you fear losing your crown, like the feeling of that crown on your head. I am a *recovering, true blue, working at never looking back- people pleaser.*

I knew people liked me, I felt loved and popular and blessed; but let me tell you, when I would find out someone *didn't* like me, or was mad at me, it would literally make me ill. I would drive myself crazy wondering why? What did I do to her? Didn't I smile at her enough? Didn't I say hi to her? I don't understand. What do I need to do? I better reach out. I better invite her over. I better get her to love me. Yuck! Yuck! Yuck!

I needed everyone to like me and if they didn't, I was miserable. And, even worse than this, if there was another girl, that seemed to be getting the attention I thought I deserved, I would compete. I am very honest about these things because I truly believe; if I get real, you get healed.

Insecurity makes us competitive in areas that are unhealthy to compete in. Saul found himself in a relationship with a man named David who started out being Saul's right hand man. He took him under his wing and David became

Saul's son, Jonathan's best friend. David was like a son to Saul. He made David the commander of his army. Whatever Saul told David to do, he did it successfully.

Then one day came when Saul and David went out to fight together, they returned to their village, and everything changed. *"When the men were returning home after David had killed the Philistine, the women came out dancing, with joyful songs and with tambourines and lutes. As they danced they sang; "Saul has slain his thousands and David his tens of thousands." Saul was very angry; this refrain galled him. "They have credited David with tens of thousands, he thought, but me with only thousands. What more can he get but the Kingdom? And from that time on Saul kept a jealous eye on David."*

Do you want to meet another ugly step cousin of insecurity? His name is jealousy. Saul's jealousy changed everything. All of the sudden his respect and appreciation for David turned into hatred. He didn't stop hating him and he ended up turning against David, chasing him, causing David to flee for his life until an actual war broke out between the house of David and the house of Saul. In 2 Samuel 3 it says that this war lasted a long time. You know when the bible says; *a long time*; now that's a long time.

Here my heart here. When your insecurity has escalated to the point of jealousy, please talk to someone about it. At least talk to God, and ask Him to heal you. Jealousy is not a safe place to be. The devil will water those insecure seeds in your heart and make you pit yourself against someone you deem as a threat, even if it is imagined.

If you don't think you struggle with a twinge of jealousy, or at least a competitive spirit, examine your heart when you are on some form of social media.

I want to be blatantly honest here, hoping to be a help and never a bearer of bad news. That newsfeed is ridden with insecurity and the pawns used in it can sometimes be our very closest loved ones.

I watch mommies compete for mother of the year on that thing. *"Behold, my 8ᵗʰ grade graduate with her medal for straight A's", "Another trip to the Zoo", "Just hanging out on the beach with my besties."* Girlfriend, I'm preaching to myself here. I know, I do it too.

But, why? Do we want the world to think we are a good mom? Do we try to get the most likes for a picture of our kids knee deep in play-dough and finger paint; so they know we aren't just lying around on the couch all day watching soap operas and eating bon-bons?

Why do we post something, then watch to see how many likes it gets, who likes it, why that same friend who we have been trying to get to like something doesn't like it? You know what I am talking about don't you?

It's insecurity my friend. It's the quick fix we are trying to get to show ourselves that people really like us, that they truly think we are good moms and we are worthy of the love we so desire. But the truth is; that it's temporal, fleeting, and goes away the next time people ignore our next post.

I stood in line with my daughter at the grocery store recently. I try not to look at the magazines that are screaming for my attention in line, but for some reason one caught my eyes, and it gave me a lump in my throat. The title said; "Best and Worst Moms". It was famous people in Hollywood with their babies, and these tabloid writers took it upon themselves to rate them as mothers. I felt so sad for them and I turned to my daughter and I said; "That's where I would draw the line if I were famous." I think it would be tough to be them hiding the plastic surgery they catch them getting, the family trips that tabloids catch them in their bathing suits looking silly, even rating the way they dress. You mess with how I mother, and it's going to hurt. And, I am sure they feel the same.

Why? Why the constant demand to compete with each other? It's exhausting. And, it is not God's will for us. God desires that we encourage each other and spur on one another towards love and good works. God's Word says; "*stop biting and devouring each other.*" We are not to be competing. We are to be loving.

Do you want to know what God is using to kill my people pleasing so that I can stay focused on being a God pleaser? He is allowing me to see that some people just don't like me. I know that this sounds strict and tough. But, the truth is; I need it.

Do you know why? Because if I continue to feed the lie inside of me that I could eventually be good enough, kind enough, helpful enough, and loving enough to get everyone to like me; I will never truly kick my people pleasing habit and I will not be able to live out God's call on my life.

God's call on my life is to follow Him, no matter the cost, and if I get tripped up trying to be all things to all people, I can't move when He says to move. My heart is to please God and I pray that people like me along the way; but guess what? If they don't, I have to forge ahead no matter what.

And, so do you!

Let's Study A Little About Jealousy:

Read the following scriptures:

- Galatians 5:19-21

- Exodus 20:17

- Ephesians 5:3-5

- 1 Corinthians 13:4-5

- 1 Corinthians 3:3

- Journal a Prayer to God asking Him to help you to abstain from jealousy of any kind:

4.

Insecurity

Saul unfortunately never got to a place of confidence. He allowed his insecurity and jealousy of David to put him at a place where he found himself consulting a witch to call on the Spirit of Samuel to pull him up to give him some advice on what to do. Saul had given up on God helping him and he sold out and reached out to a witch. The next thing we know, Saul gave up altogether and killed himself with his own sword.

Insecurity left unchecked can eventually cause you to sell out in some way, or give up all together.

We run to wrong sources as Saul did. We create idols of our own to feel better. We begin to chase money, or success, or fame, or the pursuit of beauty, or the pursuit of knowledge. We run to our cell phones to talk to someone so that we don't have to be alone in our own fears. We turn the TV on at night so we can overpower the voices that torment us. We stay plugged in all day to some sort of game or computer or social media, so that we don't have to ever feel alone.

We run! We run to sources like Saul that end up band-aiding our fears, but in the end prolong our healing. Then, sometimes just like Saul did, unfortunately, we become deceived so long by the enemy that we believe the only way out is to be done altogether.

Here me here my friend. Listen to my heart. Your last breath here on earth is not the end, it is only the beginning. You'd better make sure you never play God like Saul did and decide for yourself when enough is enough. Saul had bigger fish to fry. The second he took his last breath as a warrior, the enemy won big time.

But, not today! Say "not today!" I love how the bible says many times *"as long as it is called today."* In Hebrews it says; *"But, encourage each other daily, as long as it's called today."* Girlfriend, it's today! And, it's time for me to encourage you.

It's time for us to kick insecurities butt with a little thing I call; *"Confidence in Christ"*. Here is where it starts to get good. In preparing this chapter, I knew what I had researched, and what seemed to cause insecurity, and how becoming more confident and comfortable in our own skin we can beat insecurity; but I didn't quite know how to bridge it all for you. .I knew I wanted to bring us eventually into the New Testament where we meet grace face to face, and we see that Jesus is our healer and our redeemer and our sustainer. However I couldn't figure out how to do it. Until, God showed me.

He woke me up with the words; "Die to Saul, Live like Paul." I practically jumped out of bed to start writing, turned on the coffee pot, brushed my teeth and kept saying to myself": *Yes, die to Saul, Live like Paul."*

I've been Saul. I don't want to be like Saul ever again. So, I have to die to him and so you do. We have to learn to live like the born- again, Apostle Paul, who God gave the privilege of writing most of the New Testament: The gospel of Grace. The truth is, Paul had to also die to Saul. When God called him, his name was Saul, and God changed it to Paul. You see, God had already dealt with a Saul and that one didn't turn out very well. God gave Paul a new name when he gave him his new life in Christ.

Let me ask you something... Do you need a new name tonight? Do you need to go blind for a few days to your old self, like Paul did, before you can start seeing yourself the way God sees you? Do you need new eyes? You certainly do.

And, what can we learn from Paul? We can learn confidence, not confidence in what we can do, but confidence in what Christ can do in and through us.

In 2 Corinthians 3:4 Paul says; *"Such confidence as this is ours through Christ before God. Not that we are competent in ourselves to claim anything for ourselves, but our competence comes from God."*

Paul knew who he was before Christ called him. He was the lowliest of sinners. He was a murderer. He murdered innocent people who were worshipping and calling on the name of Christ. Paul knew that if he was to do anything out of love, peace, patience, kindness, goodness, gentleness and self-control, it would have to be by the hand of God. Paul understood and taught everyone he came in contact with that he put no confidence in the flesh. His confidence came from Christ.

Paul has this moment when I feel he is living out loud in Romans 7. I can relate to him so much here, because I have had these moments in the conflict of spiritual warfare going on so seriously inside of me that I have had to talk myself down.

It reads; *"For I have the desire to do what is good, but I can't carry it out. For what I do is not the good I want to do; no, the evil I do not want to do, I keep on doing. Now if I do what I do not want to do, it is no longer I who do it, but the sin living in me that does it."* He sort of keeps on going with this whole "who's on first routine" until he gets to the point where he says; *"who will rescue me from this body of death? Thanks be to God-Through Jesus Christ our Lord."*

Amen, my friend, Paul is pretty much saying; *"I'm nothing on my own. I am dropping the ball every time, but guess who comes to my rescue when I call on him? Jesus!"*

We need to take a lesson from Paul and talk ourselves down when we get a little insecure and frustrated with where we are. We have to remind ourselves of the truth, renew our own minds like Paul did, and talk out loud some truths to ourselves.

When we are breaking Satanic Strongholds like insecurity and jealousy, speaking truth affirmations out loud to ourselves is one of the steps to breaking these strongholds in our lives. You need to tell yourself truths from God's Word.

Truths like; *"You are more than a conqueror in Christ Jesus." "You are the righteousness of God in Christ Jesus." "You are the head and not the tail. You are above and not below."* Speak these truths to yourself when you begin to feel insecure.

Tell yourself that; *"God is with you, you are not alone, and you are loved and cherished."* You aren't going to always feel it. It doesn't matter. The truth is truth whether we can see it clearly or not and whether we feel it or no

Our feelings don't get a vote where our actions are concerned. We may not feel worthy, but God says we are worthy. We may not feel secure, but God says we are secure in Him. We may not feel loved, but God loves us. We may not feel strong but we are strong.

Paul teaches us about this strength in Philippians 4:13. It reads; *"I can do all things through Christ who gives me strength."* Girlfriend, that is not meant to be a cute magnet that we stick on the fridge. It is a life verse that we need to live out loud in front of and in spite of ourselves.

Paul says; *"Follow me as I follow Christ"*. Paul wants us to follow Him as he points our eyes upward towards a living Savior who can give us the strength we need to love when we don't feel loving, work when we don't feel like working, push when we don't feel like pushing anymore.

 The Holy Spirit gives us the strength we need to become confident in who God designed us to be. The Holy Spirit inside us confirms to us that we are not alone. In Hebrews 13: 5-6 we are reminded that God has said; *"Never will I leave you and never will I forsake you. So we say with confidence, "The Lord is my helper; I will not be afraid, what can man do to me? "*

Paul says; *"Rejoice in The Lord always, I say it again rejoice! Let your gentleness be evident to all. The Lord is near. Do not be anxious about anything, but in everything, by prayer and petition, with thanksgiving, present your requests to God. And, the peace of God which transcends all understanding will guard your hearts and minds in Christ Jesus."*

We rejoice in The Lord. The Lord is near. We give Him our everything, and He gives us His peace. .I don't know how we can lose with that deal. Our insecurity is healed by giving our fears, anxieties, and worries to God. He in turn guards our heart with that sort of protection we have always desired.

Our insecurity is healed by placing our confidence in Christ, *the author and perfecter of our faith who for the joy set before Him endured the cross.* We fix our eyes on Him, and it gets our eyes off of our weaknesses.

Our insecurity is healed by becoming a God pleaser, and not a people pleaser. Just like Paul realizes and confesses in Galatians 1:10: *"Am I now trying to win the approval of men, or of God? Or am I trying to please men? I were still trying to please men, I would not be a Servant of Christ."*

We need to cast all of our anxieties on Him, for He cares for us. My friend, God's grace is sufficient for us. His power is made perfect in our insecurities. Give Him a chance to show Himself able. Call on His grace when you are feeling weak and unable to handle the task ahead.

Come out from behind your baggage, and allow God to show you the path He has for you. His plans are to prosper you and not to harm you, plans to give you hope and a future. Stop running to wrong sources and run to the rock who is Jesus Christ.

Never be tempted to quit! It's not how we start - it's how we finish. You can finish well with Jesus at the finish line cheering you on. And, in doing all of this we will…

Die to Saul, so we can live like Paul.

Let's Study A Little About Living Like Paul:

Read the following scriptures:

- 1 Corinthians 11:1

- Romans 7:21-26

- Romans 8:37

- Philippians 4:13

- Philippians 4:4-9

- Journal a prayer to God asking Him to help you die to Saul and live like Paul:

What You Are Worth

Posted on August 21, 2012 by momydlo@wordpress.com

I went out to the mailbox today and I found a letter from the taxing authority with the latest assessment of our house, and how much they have decided our house is worth right now. Yes, we need assessments to determine fair market values of homes, but how about fair family value of the home? Does that get considered?

Does the government take into account how many Fourth of July picnics we have hosted here with friends and family all around us? Do they count how many lost teeth have made their way under pillows here, in great expectation of the tooth fairy? Do they count how many hours of homework and bible studies have taken place in our living room? Do they estimate the food costs of the dinners that we have eaten together around the table as a family? Do they count how many times we have put up and taken down the Christmas decorations and ornaments as a family? Do they count how many times I have stood in the driveway waiting as the bus brings my babies home from school?

Who decides what the worth and value of our home is? I think it is our family. I think the worth and value of your home should be determined by the amount of memories you have created behind those four walls.

Who gets to decide your worth and value? A report card? A diploma? A "dream job"? How many kids you have? How many possessions you have acquired? Who decides?

The Grace Race

Our worth and value does not come from any of this. It doesn't come from who we are, or what we do, or who knows us. It comes from WHOSE we are.

When you have made Jesus Christ the Lord of your life, you belong to God. You are joint heirs with Christ and you are the Righteousness of God in Christ Jesus.

Your worth and value does not come from anything you have done or ever will do. It comes from being adopted into the family of God because of what our Savior did for us!

Let's Study A Little About Our Worth In Christ:

Read the following scriptures:

- 2 Corinthians 5:17

- Romans 8:17

- Romans 8:37

- Acts 1:8

- 1 John 4:4

- Journal a Prayer to God asking Him to help you remember how valuable you are to Him, and to the Kingdom of God:

Paul Gets Real!

Posted on August 16, 2013 by momydlo

This morning I was studying on my back porch, just enjoying the still of the morning and the taste of my black coffee. It was so dark that I kept turning my bible upward to catch the only light from one of my exterior porch lights. I knew God must have wanted to show me something, as I really could have used a couple more minutes sleep, but He is worth it!

I was reading my devotionals and one of them took me to Philippians. I was reading in chapter 2 where Paul is talking about shining like stars in a crooked world. He is talking to the Christians in Philippi about keeping a good attitude and not grumbling and complaining. I was immediately convicted.

Oh…I can overdo it with home repairs and cleaning and then complain in the evening when I ache. I can overbook myself down to 15 minute increments and then take deep breaths when my pop-tarts take too long to cook in the toaster. I can tell my kids to go play, then walk in a room full of toys an hour later and say; "what bomb went off in here?" Yes, I was immediately convicted.

Then, I felt like God gave me a mulligan. (For those who don't know golf-that's a second chance.) It was like a "Hang in there Mo… keep doing your best. Even giants in the faith like Paul were still human." I kept reading to find Paul having what I would call "a moment". Here he was just talking to the saints in Philippi about their attitudes. Then a couple scriptures later he tells them he is sending his friend Epaphroditus back home to them because he knows he longs to go home to his friends and family in Philippi. However, Paul doesn't just say; "My friends, rejoice because Epaphroditus is coming home." He gets in a little dig when he tells them of his friend's return. In verse 2:29-30 Paul says; "Welcome him in The Lord with great joy, and honor men like him, because he almost died for the work of Christ, risking his life to **make up for the help that you could not give me.**"

Ooh, Paul is playing the martyr here, just like I have done many times. He had felt a little let down by the people that he thought should have been helping him, so he gave them a little love…with a side order of guilt! Hmm….sound familiar? It does because we all do it. When the expectations that we set aren't met in our minds, we often grumble, complain, or maybe just give people some attitude.

Why do we forget that these men who we read about in the bible were simply… MEN? We are all imperfect, flawed, humans, daily in need of a Savior's touch. When we get an inch too far from Jesus, we act like the fool.

I think Paul may have been ministering to himself when he was telling the crowd to not grumble and complain because usually the things that we are preaching, we have experienced ourselves. Paul was probably fighting arguing and complaining in his own heart, so he was trying to help others at the same time.

Do yourself a favor and don't put bible teachers, Pastors, and church leaders on a pedestal. We are all a bunch of hot messes, just desperate for Jesus, just like you! Yes, I think I like Paul even more now! Let's get real, so we can get healed!

Let's Study A Little About Grumbling and Complaining:

Read the following scriptures:

- Exodus 16:8

- Philippians 2:14

- Ephesians 4:29

- James 5:9

- Journal a prayer to God asking Him to help you to keep a good attitude, as well as not expect anyone here on earth to be perfect, no matter what his title or occupation is:

5.

Grace

Grace is huge! Grace is everything; because my friends. Jesus is grace, and Jesus is everything! This is a grace gospel. Let's read what Paul says in Galatians 1:6: *"I am astonished that you are so quickly deserting the one who called you by the grace of Christ and are turning to a different gospel-which is really no gospel at all.."*(my words here ladies…gospel means good news. Paul is saying, what you are turning to here, is not good news). *Evidently some people are throwing you into confusion and are trying to pervert the gospel of Christ. But even if we or an angel from Heaven* (here are my words again ladies, or a Pastor you really trust) *should preach a gospel other than the one we preached to you, let him be eternally condemned. As we have already said, so now I say again; if anybody is preaching to you a gospel other than what you accepted, let him be eternally condemned."* Am I now trying to win the approval of men, or of God? Or am I trying to please men? If I were trying to please men, I would not be a servant of Christ."

Ok, first I say; Confession time; It's scary being a teacher. Teachers are held very accountable in God's eyes. It's almost as if He says to us; "get it, or get out! Don't mess up what I am trying to tell them, and don't worry about what people will say about my truth. Just tell the truth!"

Paul is adamant that we understand the gospel of grace and never turn back to other methods of living and teaching. Why? Because this one is God's: This one is the true gospel. this one is the good news; And, this one my friend, cost God His son. It cost Him everything, and He is serious about honoring His son's blood and sacrifice. God is serious about Grace.

I think God was teaching me a lesson in an incident this month as I was preparing this chapter to see how far I would go for Him? Wow, did I have to fight old people pleasing habits. I had to keep reminding myself that I am a God pleaser and not a people pleaser and I think God was using that lesson to strengthen me for tonight.

 You see, you aren't necessarily going to agree with everything I tell you, because in many of us, ingrained in our being is this "Inner Pharisee" that loves to point out the sin in everyone around us, to try to get eyes off of ourselves. I am probably going to push every legalistic button you have right here in this last chapter; so here goes. I hope you still love me after. Because I have to preach grace. Paul demands it, and so does God.

We have to be real to get healed. We have to be ready to say with Godly confidence; "If not but for the grace of God, this would be my life."

Just a couple days ago I had dinner with some of my sweetest friends in the faith. We found ourselves talking like this, saying; "Thank you Jesus you rescued me from this…, and it's only by the grace of God that I was saved from that…" We were discussing stories of sin, and danger, and poor decisions and so much more. And, these women were in the ministry, amen?

God's grace saved us from Hell. God's grace delivers us from death daily. What Jesus did for us on the cross once and for all, mean everything to us.

I think that any good speaker or presenter getting ready to give a topical message or speech knows that a good dictionary definition of a topic is always a smart place to start. So here goes. I looked up Grace.

At dictionary.com I looked up grace and I found 5 different definitions.

1) Elegance of beauty or form, manner or measure. This definition could refer to the grace of a ballerina, or maybe a dancer who just seems to be light on her feet, and hit every step.
2) An attractive or pleasing quality. (this definition could be used to say like someone is filled with social graces. When I think of this, I picture the first class passengers on the Titanic. Hold the pinky up at the table, know which fork is for the salad, and which is for dinner. Not, country girls like me so much.
3) Here's where I think it gets good…the third definition of grace is favor or goodwill. That one speaks for itself. It is simply kindness. It's simply showing kindliness to someone. This is the love your neighbor stuff, showing kindness to someone just because.

4) Fourth definition; a manifestation of favor, especially by a superior. This one involves forgiveness, charity, mercifulness. This is the gift bestowed upon you, deserved, or undeserved…

5) Mercy, clemency, pardon…This definition means everything to us. This definition is what secures our salvation.

And, this was just from dictionary.com

Wanna hear Webters?……this made me laugh;

Definition of *GRACE*

1

a: unmerited divine assistance given humans for their regeneration or sanctification

b: a virtue coming from God

c: a state of sanctification enjoyed through divine grace

2

a: APPROVAL, FAVOR <stayed in his good *graces*>

barchaic: MERCY, PARDON

c: a special favor : PRIVILEGE <each in his place, by right, not *grace*, shall rule his heritage — Rudyard Kipling>

d: disposition to or an act or instance of kindness, courtesy, or clemency

e: a temporary exemption : REPRIEVE

3

a: a charming or attractive trait or characteristic

b: a pleasing appearance or effect : CHARM <all the *grace* of youth — John Buchan>

c: ease and suppleness of movement or bearing

4

—used as a title of address or reference for a duke, a duchess, or an archbishop

5

: a short prayer at a meal asking a blessing or giving thanks

6

pluralcapitalized: three sister goddesses in Greek mythology who are the givers of charm and beauty

7

: a musical trill, turn, or appoggiatura

8

a: sense of propriety or right <had the *grace* not to run for elective office — Calvin Trillin>

b: the quality or state of being considerate or thoughtful

See grace defined for English-language learners »

See grace defined for kids »

Do you know what this research showed me my friend? If the people who write dictionaries are confused with the word grace, no wonder we as Christians are confused with the biblical concept of grace.

Travel with me somewhere quickly; Guess who the bible refers to as the author of confusion? Satan! If the enemy can keep us confused about grace, and what it actually covers and what it means to us, we can become weak and powerless.

When you lack wisdom, the bible says ask God. We have to go to God's Word to see how God defines grace. My concordance is simply put; Grace; "God's free and unmerited favor for sinful humanity." Thank you Jesus for simplicity. I am not a wordsmith my friends. I need straight forward truth. It's God's gift to sinners! It's God's power given to us.

Grace is God's power to conquer the grave and take away the power of sin and death once and for all. God's grace had to come, simply because even after we knew what sin was, we were still unable to conquer it.

Here's a little history for you my friends. From the time of Adam to Moses people would sin, not even knowing it was sin. There was no order to follow or rules to stay within. Therefore God knew He had to send a law to the people so that they would be conscious of sin. If there was no sign anywhere and you don't know how fast you are going, you just speed and you don't feel guilty right? But, as soon as we see that sign, our brain says; *"Ok, slow down, follow the speed limit,* (well, usually)."

The Ten Commandments were sent, to show people what sin was.

God sent his perfect law to earth, and under this original covenant when you were obedient to the law, you were blessed, when you broke the law, you were cursed.

When God presented the law to Moses and the Israelites were given the original perfect law, with all of it's stipulations. God then told them how to build the tabernacle, and the ark, and how to carry it, who can carry it, etc. Guess what God ordered of them next? Offerings and sacrifices. The book of Leviticus is filled with different sacrifices and offerings needed to offer up to God. He did this because He knew they were unable to keep the law, and in God's eyes, breaking part of the law, meant you broke the entire law. God doesn't grade on a curve my friend. Sin is sin in God's eyes. Say that with me; "Sin is sin!"

This original covenant that God made with his people was perfect. Don't misunderstand me; but this law was given to let humanity know we are sinners, in need of a Savior.

It's always been about Jesus, only about Jesus and all about Jesus. Jesus was God's plan A. The law was given to bring humanity to an end of themselves; to realize they were helpless to follow this Holy Law completely and to point sinners towards a Savior.

God didn't send the law to make us holy. The law is holy, but we aren't. The law was like a mirror into our sinfulness. When you look into a mirror, it is just a reflection of you. You can't take the mirror off the wall and change yourself with it. It just shows the real you. The law showed people their sins. It didn't make them holy.

In the old covenant; God had to give his children a chance to make offerings and sacrifices so that they could have a temporary relief from their guilt. The law always reminded them of their guilt because they couldn't keep it perfectly, hence the need for the guilt offerings.

When Jesus came; He became our final, perfect, spotless, offering whose blood would be the atonement for our sins once and for all. The blood of Jesus opens up the door for God's grace to flow in our lives.

You see, all throughout the Old Testament, the prophets and the people had no other choice but to look to the law, work to follow and abide by the law, and offer sacrifices according to the law so as to rest in the blessing of God. That was the original covenant God made with his people.

Obedience to the law brought blessing, breaking the law brought curses. Then, when Jesus showed up, everything changed. Jesus' death on the cross changed everything. His life and death perfectly fulfilled the law once and for all, atoning for our inability to ever do so.

Matthew; 5; 17-20 reads; *"Do not think I have come to abolish the law or the prophets; I have come to fulfill them. I tell you the truth, until Heaven and earth disappear, not the smallest letter not the least stroke of a pen, will be any means disappear from the Law until everything is accomplished. Anyone who breaks one of the least of these commandments and teaches others to do the same will be called least in the Kingdom of Heaven, but whoever practices and teaches these commands will be called great in the Kingdom of Heaven. For I tell you, that unless your righteousness surpasses that of the Pharisees and the teachers of the law, you will certainly not enter the Kingdom of God."*

Jesus is saying; see these Pharisees, they are adamant about the law. They are pretty much completely and undeniably law minded, they think about it daily, minute by minute, hour by hour, trying striving to be perfect, and Jesus says; It's not enough. They can't do it. It's too perfect. He is showing them; Your righteousness has to surpass that.

What is righteousness? Righteousness is right standing with God. How do we attain that? We wear robes of righteousness once we are baptized into Christ. Here it is again, your ability to stand righteous in front of God, depends on Jesus' sacrifice and His blood. Jesus paid it all, and we owe Him everything!

We are no longer under the old covenant. We are new covenant believers, and the new covenant is the new covenant of grace.

In the old covenant, both the people and God had a part. The law told you what to do in order for God to do something. The new covenant; God decided to sort of make a covenant with Himself by sending Jesus to be our High Priest. He knew we couldn't keep our part of the agreement, so He made a covenant with himself.

I was meditating on this one day after I had studied it out until my mind was aching. I decided to go throw in a load of laundry. I had to walk away from my computer and books for a minute.

I started to think about covenant relationships and our relationship with God, our husbands, and with our families. As I was thinking about it, I was folding laundry. I thought; *"that's it! I have made a laundry covenant with my kids."* My kids part in the laundry covenant is to dirty the clothes, sometimes bring the dirty clothes into the laundry room, and when clean clothes are sitting on the end of their bed, they are supposed to put these clothes away (within a reasonable time frame).

My part in the laundry covenant is; to sort the clothes, wash the clothes, fold the clothes and lovingly put the clothes on the end of their beds.

Do my kids keep their end of the covenant relationship? Not always, but sometimes they do. Yes, I usually have to convict them, remind them that they left their dirty underwear in the bathroom after their shower, and it wasn't fun for me to pick them up before my small group showed up for bible study. Sometimes even after I have given them deadlines and said; *"If you don't put your clothes away this evening you can't go to the mall with Uncle Rob."* I walk in the room the next morning and the clean clothes are still all over the floor and closet. Well, then I have to discipline.

Even though my kids know the rules and they know their part of the laundry covenant; they don't always keep theirs. But, I have decided to keep my end. I pour out a heaping of grace on them, and I keep my end of the laundry covenant. Why? Because I have made a separate covenant with myself that my kids aren't wearing dirty clothes to school….and my kids are not going to be the *smelly* kids if I have anything to do with it! Sometimes if I am in a grace filled mood, I will even go in and hang up some of their clothes and pray for them as I do so, not because I have to ladies, but because I love them, and I want them to understand grace. *Plus, I just like my house clean.* Do you get my point?

God knew the first covenant that He made before Jesus came wasn't working. God's kids were walking around like the *smelly* kids. God knew He needed to send grace so that we could even hang around Him, spend time with Him, and glorify Him. We couldn't do it on our own. We needed Grace. We needed Jesus!

The law brought death. When the original law was presented on Mount Sinai, 3000 people died in their sin. When the Holy Spirit came on the believers at Pentecost, 3000 people were saved. God sent the Holy Spirit to us so that we could have life and have it in abundance, until it overflowed. Are we blessed or what?

The old covenant was written on tablets of stone. The new covenant of

Grace is written on our hearts. We are going to read; Hebrews 8:7. Now, before we get started, let me create the scenario. The writer of Hebrews has just explained that Jesus is our new High Priest. In the old covenant, the High Priest was the only one allowed each year behind the curtain of the Holy of Holies. He would go in and offer sacrifices for the people for their guilt. Now, they had to do this over and over and over, because it is impossible for the blood of lambs and goats to totally take away sin. Now, with Jesus as our High Priest, He sits at the right hand of the throne of God interceding for us daily. That is acting as our Holy Lawyer my friend, saying; *God, forgive them; according to what I have done.* Because Jesus is now our High Priest. When God looks at us, He sees His son and His sacrifice. His blood covers us.

Hebrews 8:7: "For if there had been nothing wrong with the first covenant, no place would have been sought for another. But, God found fault with the people and said; "The time is coming, declares the Lord when I will make a new covenant with the house of Israel and with the house of Judah. It will not be like the covenant I made with their forefathers when I took them by the hand to lead them out of Egypt because they did not remain faithful to my covenant, and I turned away from them. This is the covenant I will make with the house of Israel after that time, declares the Lord. I will put my laws in their minds and write them on their hearts. I will be their God, and they will be my people. No longer will a man teach his neighbor or a man his brother saying, "Know the Lord," because they will all know me, from the least to the greatest. For I will forgive their wickedness and will remember their sins no more." By calling this covenant "new", he has made the first one obsolete, and what is obsolete and aging, will soon disappear."

When you make Jesus your Lord; when you recognize Him as your high priest; when you become covered with His righteousness at the time of your new birth as a baptized believer; God writes His laws on your heart.

He sends us The Mighty Counselor, the Holy Spirit, to help us to follow his commandments. We no longer have to be told and taught over and over what laws we are messing up, breaking, and missing the mark on. We are guided by The Holy Spirit... God's Spirit on the inside of us.

Understand this and figure this out once and for all; God's new covenant of Grace gives us the power to fight sin once and for all in our lives.

God's grace gives us power. God's grace does not give us a license to sin. God's grace in our lives gives us the power and the favor that we need to not sin.

You will hear legalistic people say to pastors; *"OH, you better not preach too much on grace, because people will just think they can just keep sinning and they will be forgiven no matter what. "*

Girlfriend, guess what? You are going to sin, no matter what. If you think you can do it alone without grace, you are greatly mistaken. You can't follow God's perfect law without grace.

God did not just save us by grace just to give us eternal salvation when we die. God has granted us his grace so that we can conquer sin in our lives while we are here.

Also, I would even venture to say; that the more you keep your eyes on following the law, doing good, not messing up, trying to work yourself crazy thinking you will earn right standing with God and getting into self-protect mode, you are more apt to sin. Because hey, guess what; worry is sin. Woops, there you go. You broke the perfect law, trying to keep the law.

Let me explain. The enemy of your soul has much to gain with you believing that God's grace can't help keep you from sinning. If he can lie to you enough saying; *"you're gonna mess up, your gonna screw up. You can't possibly be righteous, just look at what you have done, think what you think like...."* And, if that enemy can get you to start believing that if you do enough good, it might be able to negate some of the bad you have done in the past. He can get you on that treadmill of a works- based religion, and you will take your eyes off our perfect sacrifice Jesus Christ who has been there all along, saying; *"It's done, I've already done it. It's finished."*

Hebrews 4:8 says; "Blessed is the man whose sin the Lord will never count against him." My friend, that scripture screams grace.

In Romans 6: 18 it reads; *"Consequently, just as the result of one trespass was condemnation for all men,* (the bible is talking about Adam here, when sin started in the garden), *so also the result of one act of righteousness was justification that brings life for all men."* And, that's Jesus my friend, That's Grace Himself.

We are not under the law anymore, we are under grace. We are dead to sin. Grace gives us the power to say no to sin. We are no longer slaves to sin. Focusing on God's grace does not give us a license to sin. It gives us the power not to.

In Romans 6:1-7 it reads; *"What shall we say then? Shall we go on sinning so that grace may increase? By no means! We died to sin; how can we live in it any longer? Or don't you know that all of us who were baptized into Christ Jesus were baptized into his death? We therefore were buried with him through baptism into death, that just as Christ was raised from the dead through the glory of the Father, we too may live a new life. If we have been united with him like this in his death, we will certainly also be united with him in his resurrection. For we know that our old self was crucified with him so that the body of sin might be done away with, that we should no longer be slaves to sin- because anyone who has died has been freed from sin."*

Say this with me my friend; *"I'm dead to sin."* God's grace releases us from being slaves to sin. Will we still sin while we are under grace? We sure will! But the bible says; *where sin abounds, grace abounds much more.*

Your sins of the past, your sins today, and your sins in the future, are covered under the blood of Jesus. God's Word says; *He has forgiven our wickedness and our sins He will remember no more.* Why? Because God's grace causes Him to look at Jesus when He looks at us.

In the Old Testament God had much wrath. He was seldom able to bless His people because of their unrighteousness. But, under the new covenant of grace, His Word says in Romans 5:9: *"Since we have now been justified by his blood, how much more shall we be saved from God's wrath through Him."* The truth is; God poured out His wrath on His son at the cross so we would not have to suffer His wrath. God forsook His son, so that we can be Unforsaken! He paid it all my friend! Grace paid it all. Can you say amen?

Grace is unmerited favor. Unmerited, means undeserved. But, God gave it to us anyways. Grace means power, power to overcome the enemies schemes to get you to believe you have to sin. You are dead to sin and alive to righteousness. You are slaves to righteousness now.

Grace helps us get our minds off our sin and get our minds on our righteousness. We need to tell ourselves over and over until we believe it; *"I am the righteousness of God in Christ Jesus.*" You are righteous only because of, always because of and forever because of, our High Priest Jesus.

We need to get a little grace minded. We need to get a little excited about what Grace means. Grace means we have the power to fight habits; we have the power to fight strongholds; and we have the power to fight sickness, disease, poverty, depression, anxiety, worry, and many others.

Don't those things make you feel weak? You know what Paul says about that in 2 Corinthians 12: He is pleading with God to take away the thorn in his flesh, this annoying messenger from Satan to torment him. What God s tells him is priceless for us to remember; "*My grace is sufficient for you. My power is made perfect in weakness.*"

When we are weak, we are strong! Yes, because when we are weak, grace shows up. Let me tell you something that I have noticed about God. He is very close to the broken hearted. When you are going through something very difficult, sometimes it is amazing what supernatural peace you have while going through this trial that literally should bring you to your knees. Do you know where that strength comes from? It's God's Grace.

God's grace is sufficient for us when we are struggling. When we stay occupied with Jesus, with His righteousness and His provision, with His protection and His strength, we are strong.

We are new covenant believers. I know I said earlier that God sort of made a covenant with Himself so that whether we did our part or not, He would be faithful. But, the truth is, just like my kids had a part to play with the laundry, we have a part as well. It's the same thing that brought blessing in the old covenant, it's obedience. This obedience is not obedience to the law my friend. The law is written on our hearts now and grace helps us to fulfill it.

The obedience required of us is obedience to the faith. In Romans 1:5-6 it reads; "*Through Him and for His name's sake, we received grace and apostleship to call people from among the gentiles to the obedience that comes from faith. And you also are among those who are called to belong to Jesus Christ.*"

Obedience to the faith means that we belong to Jesus Christ. We belong to Him because we are now slaves to righteousness. Slaves have a biblical responsibility to submit to their master. Being a slave to righteousness means we follow the leading of The Holy Spirit.

Let's decide what our master Jesus Christ wants from us so that we can be obedient. Travel with me to Matthew 28: 18; At this point in the gospel Jesus has walked the earth, taught the disciples, died on the cross, rose again and has returned to the disciples to give them final instructions, before He returned to the Father.

It reads: *"Then Jesus came to them and said; "All authority in heaven and earth has been given to me. Therefore, go and make disciples of all nations, baptizing them in the name of the Father, and of the Son, and of The Holy Spirit, and teaching them to obey everything I have commanded you. And, surely I am with you always to the very end of the age."*

Our part in the covenant relationship is to let the world know about Jesus! Our part in the covenant relationship is to teach others about the gospel of grace. What does Jesus promise at the end? He promised that He will be with us the whole time. Amen! We are Unforsaken! He isn't going to leave us to venture alone. He will walk with us step by step, guiding us by The Holy Spirit.

So, really, the only way that we are not keeping up the covenant relationship with God is if we are secretive about our faith. If you say; *"oh, I'm very private about my beliefs."* You're in disobedience. If we are private about our faith how can we share Jesus with others? How can we make sure that each and every person that we love is guaranteed a ticket into Heaven if we don't tell them about the only way there? Jesus says; *"I am the way, the truth and the life, no one comes to The Father except through me."*

If you never share Christ with another person after you get saved; who have you stolen from? They need a chance to receive that gift of grace as well. Whose name will not be written in the lamb's book of life because you didn't share with them? If you don't keep your part of the new covenant of grace which is obedience to the faith, who loses? We need to have a holy ambition burning on the inside of us at every minute to see our loved ones saved. We need to constantly be asking God, *"Ok, who can I love today in your name? Who are you aching to embrace Lord? I am your slave Lord. I am a slave to righteousness."*

You see, everything that we are given from God, He expects us to be prepared to give it away. His Word says; *"Freely you have received, freely give."* God has given us His grace so that we can be grace givers.

When Grace shows up:

We can say no to sin.

When Grace shows up:

We can conquer the enemy's attacks

When Grace shows up:

We can put the past to death once and for all.

When Graces shows up:

We can get excited about our future in Christ.

When Grace shows up:

People can get saved.

When Grace shows up:

We are free to love.

Let's pray; Heavenly Father, In the name of Jesus we thank you. We thank you for your unmerited favor poured out on us. Lord, we thank you for saving us when we make Jesus Lord of our lives. We thank you that because of your grace we are able to stay in the race. Lord we thank you for your forgiveness.

Girlfriend; You are Unforsaken! Stay in the race relying heavily on grace!

The Grace Race

About The Author

Mo Mydlo has been happily married to Tommy Mydlo for twenty years. They reside in the Central Florida area with their four children and their dog Tyco. Mo was ordained into ministry and served for six years as the Outreach Director for one of the fastest growing churches in the nation.

Mo is passionate about teaching women how to renew their minds in The Word of God. Mo is the Director for a Non-Profit Corporation called; The Vineyard-A Single Moms Community. The Vineyard is actively establishing and building a community for single moms and their kids. Mo also teaches and directs an Interdenominational Community Bible Study/Women's Event called; Unforsaken Women.

Mo is available to speak at women's groups, workshops, events, churches, and retreats. For more information about her schedule, please visit her website; www.unforsakenministries.com

You can also follow Mo on Twitter, Facebook, Youtube.com and Wordpress.com

Other Books By Mo

Notes From A Titus Woman; The A-Z of Caring for Your Home and
Family
Available on amazon.com

I Go Before You
A Companion For Your Journey Through Emotional Healing
Available at amazon.com

Overcoming Anxiety Biblically
Available at amazon.com

Overcoming Anxiety Biblically; A Leader's Guide
Available at amazon.com

Keepin' It Real
Available at amazon.com

Perfect Love
Available at amazon.com

I would love to hear from you on your experience with this book.

Please contact me on my website;
www.unforsakenministries.com

 Follow me on Facebook; Unforsaken by Mo Mydlo

 Follow me on Twitter

 Follow me on my blog; momydlo@wordpress.com

The Grace Race

Made in the USA
Middletown, DE
17 March 2022

62771804R00066